Woman@Heart

Essays on life, love, laughter and tears

Claire Yezbak Fadden

Cover by Selestiele Designs
Editor: Barb Wilson
Published by Brightwood Books
Formatted by Enterprise Book Services, LLC

978-0-9988645-3-2

To the men in my life, Nick, Shawn, Jake and Seth.

My inspiration, my fodder, my truest fans.

WOMAN WISE

Claire Yezbak Fadden

THE FAMILY FRONT

Get the Picture

Under a crisp, sunny summer sky, serious faces study programs, debate odds and circle sure winners in the racing form. There were a few minutes to post as my family mills around, each one with an ink pen at the ready. It's our annual *Uncle George Day* at the horse races. This group of about twenty is focused on how to parlay two dollars into two hundred. Everyone, that is, except me. My winning ticket involves capturing this moment with one snap of my digital camera.

Corralling chickens is easier.

Hours earlier, we set up lawn chairs and spread blankets on the trackside apron in preparation for a picnic of sandwiches, fruit, and chips. Gathered alongside my husband Nick and my sons Shawn, Jake, and Seth are sisters, brothers, uncles, aunts, nieces, nephews, cousins and longtime friends. None are interested in the future importance of photos chronicling our outing to where the turf meets the surf. More attention is paid to an oversized bag of kettle corn propped against the cooler.

Nonetheless, I remain undaunted and perhaps a tad annoying. It's not every day this group, spread over hundreds of miles, is together. Hoping to placate me—and have a chance to get their bets in before the windows close—people slowly shifted into frame. A few even smiled. I smiled back as I take the picture.

"Oh, don't move," I said. And the voice of any one of my sons replied, "We've got to take two."

With the images safely stored on my flash drive, everyone moved to their original places. The sound of a trumpet played in the distance. A few scurried to the betting windows, seemingly mesmerized by names like Briarpatch Betty, Countyourwinnings and Pappaspepper. The younger kids scampered toward the metal fence surrounding the track and watched the horses and their jockeys trot to the starting gate. I breathed a sigh. Another family memory captured for eternity.

My gang hasn't realized it yet, but someday these random snapshots converted to digital data will become family treasures. We moms *know*. That's why many of us assumed the role of family photographer/historian, with the same seamless leadership and commitment we exhibited as family party planner, nutritionist, and chauffeur. And this usually means we're not in the picture—at least most of the time. That's a small price to pay in exchange for the satisfaction of having the images of those we love preserved on a sheet of photo paper, tucked into a family album or captured on a computer slide show.

I wasn't always a fan of digital photography. I mistrusted anything I couldn't drop off at the drugstore for developing. It took nearly a year after receiving a digital camera from my husband for Christmas before I traded in my insecure attachment of film rolls for the convenience, efficiency, and quality of a digicam. I fell in love with knowing instantaneously whether the photo was good or not. No more waiting days or weeks to find out I had blinked, someone had looked away, or one of my sons (or their pals) had photo-bombed the picture.

Later that day, while everyone else gathered around the dining room table recapping their winners and losers, I snuck off to my computer to download the candid shots snapped in between races. I lingered a moment and after a few mouse clicks, I opened a digital slide show of other family events.

One son's first day at kindergarten, their grandmother's 80th birthday, the sweet smile of a new bride. It doesn't matter where the pictures are stored—in an album, on a hard drive or at a photo-sharing site. Or whether my face is in the group smiling from the image. I'm part of the moment and the emotion that only a photo can preserve.

I smiled as the images glided past, reminding me of forgotten occasions. Like the Saturday morning I had awoken everyone early for a family portrait. The professional photographer insisted the light at the beach was best before the clouds vanished, sometime around seven a.m. Complaints and protests—mostly Nick's— echoed in my ears.

"Why are we up earlier than the sun?" he asked, as he and our sons trudged barefoot through the sand to reach a seawall.

Wearing rolled-up jeans and white T-shirts, our fivesome posed casually, while the photographer captured our smiles forever. It's a great portrait.

And this time, I'm in the picture.

Spring Cleaning

Somewhere in the Laguna Mountains, the frost is melting. The anticipated warmth will bring a bumper crop of bunnies, chicks, and baby deer. My daffodil bulbs were in the ground and I'm awaiting their buttery yellow blooms in the next couple weeks. Soon butterflies and ladybugs will skitter through my backyard. I felt invigorated at the prospect of new beginnings, fresh starts, clean slates. I marvel at the outdoors, ready to burst with new life.

For me, though, it's the crowded indoors—specifically my cabinets, closets, and storage shelves—that are busting out all over. I feared that one more windbreaker, jacket, or muffler hooked onto my entryway coat rack will topple it over like a poorly played Jenga game. The hall closet's sagging wardrobe pole was a hoodie away from snapping, and there was nowhere to wedge another forgotten golf club, baseball mitt, or shin guard into the under-the-staircase closet.

With five people living under one roof, lots of can't-live-without possessions seeped into our home over the years, found a cozy nook, and made themselves comfortable. Hardly noticing new belongings had arrived, I just scooted, squeezed, and crammed a bit more into our finite space. It wasn't until I knocked over a glass trying to put my Best Mom coffee mug back in the cupboard that I realized even a Dixie cup wouldn't fit on the shelf. To open up space, I toyed briefly with relocating some of my dishes to the pantry, but there wasn't any room in there either.

I admired women who seamlessly kept clutter to a minimum. With their family's blessing and support, they implemented organizational plans, strategies, and charts. They wouldn't be making a guest appearance on a TV show about hoarders. In my campaign to be counted among them, last year I adopted a policy: New One In-Old One Out. Now, every time I added a blouse or dress to my stash, I eagerly donated a gently worn one to the local women's shelter or charity.

I was always on the hunt for other stuff to recycle, too. If I could repurpose one extraneous thing a day, by the end of the year, I will have reclaimed area currently occupied by 365 dust catchers, neglected toys, and underused garments. I kept a carton in the corner of my garage to corral donations. At the moment it held a couple cell phone cases, a deep fryer, four plastic baseball cap bowls and two pairs of sneakers.

I'm about forty-seven items behind schedule.

Obviously, I'm not the one who's afraid to remove stuff. It's my family who can't let go. And when you're outnumbered four to one (counting my husband Nick), it's nearly impossible to streamline. I've pleaded, cajoled, and threatened my fab four in the hopes of igniting their urge to purge, all to no avail. They liked cramming more into their closets and dresser drawers. It's gotten so bad that my laundry baskets now doubled as portable chifforobes.

I haven't given up, though. Recently, I introduced my own clutter-clearing idea: the S.T.U. Clothing Exchange Program. To qualify for new Socks, T-shirts and Underwear, the owner must relinquish a threadbare, hole-y one of similar design. No turning in your brother's soccer shorts, or Dad's baseball shirt for credit toward a new pair of boxers.

I've been tempted—when they aren't looking—to toss out some of their excess, but I stink at stealth operations. So yesterday, in the spirit of spring cleaning, I confronted them in their rooms—Salvation Army donation bag clutched in hand—and began filling it, forcing Nick and my sons Jake and Seth to defend what they truly wanted to keep and to sacrifice the stuff they'd forgotten they had.

My oldest son Shawn has moved out of the family home. A lot of his belongings have not. Boxes of mementos, trophies, and other memorabilia too precious for him to discard (or take with him) lived on in my closet shelves, bookcases, and corners of the garage.

I understood Shawn's attachment, though. I hung on to stuff I might never use again, like a dog-eared copy of *The Poky Little Puppy*, or the orange-colored cotton apron my mom sewed in her junior-high home ec class. Baby teeth, grade-school award programs, all-star jackets, and a wedding dress were safely tucked inside my hope chest.

Clearly, I'm onboard with protecting cherished bits and pieces of the past. It's the unmatched soccer socks, outgrown sweatpants and soda can koozies I wanted relocated to new digs. Well, maybe next year.

The Best of Buddies

My family was standing near the avocado trees in a corner of our back yard. There was whispered conversation, muffled sniffles. Lots of eyes stared at the ground. Occasionally, a finger moved to wipe away tears as they trailed down a cheek. Nick stood off to the side holding a shovel.

It's not the first time this solemn-faced group had gathered like this. The seven of us (including family friends Lisa and Rachel) stood in this same spot two years ago to say good-bye to Max, our soccer-ball-chasing terrier-spaniel mix. He'd joined our family sixteen years ago after my oldest son Shawn and then-toddler Seth picked him out as a surprise for their brother Jake's seventh birthday. My sons fell in love after watching this four-legged black fur ball toss a soccer ball in the air with his nose, then chase after it.

Today it's Seth's turn to say good-bye to Baylor, his childhood pet of nine years. Although he loved Max, when Seth was ten, he mounted a campaign for a dog of his own. He argued a strong case, too, relying heavily on Max's obsession to escape the confines of our home. Next to eating snails, plotting backyard breakouts was Max's favorite pastime.

"He's here all day by himself," Seth said, playing the loneliness angle. "Max wouldn't try to get out of the backyard if he had a buddy." To seal the deal, Seth pledged to feed, scoop, and walk his future pet.

So, seven years later, we returned from the animal shelter with a playmate for Max—a five-year-old beagle mix. There were many pets to choose from, but one stood out from the pack. As Seth approached, Baylor introduced himself by standing on his back legs and using his front ones, he hugged this potential owner-to-be around the waist. When Seth hugged back, I knew he was hooked.

In truth, so was I.

Our caramel-colored dog came equipped with chocolate brown eyes, a tire-tread-marked broken tail (that we had docked) and a bit of emotional baggage. He was skittish, submissive, and in the beginning, sat with his back against a wall so nothing—or no one—could sneak up from behind. Instead of chasing a kicked soccer ball, Baylor would run to get out of the way. He was a lover, not a sportsman.

On lazy afternoons, he'd lay his head on your lap, waiting for a rubdown. If you stopped too soon, Baylor nuzzled your hand as if to say, "Continue, please." Max stopped burrowing for an exit and the pair became best friends. At fifteen years old (that's 105 for you and me), it was time for Baylor to join Max in doggie heaven.

In the coolness of a Saturday morning, we waited for Seth who stood in the middle of the semi-circle, head tilted down, clutching a paving stone. Fighting to keep his composure, he read the words he chose:

Baylor. A big buddy with an even bigger heart.

Seth used his fingers to wipe the plaque clean and then knelt down to lay the stone on the freshly turned soil. Inches away, another marker reads: *Max. A wise friend and the best buddy.*

With the short ceremony over, the group turned around to see a duo of curious onlookers—Bandit and Jersey Girl, our newest pet members. About a year ago, we discovered Bandit, a rat terrier, at the same animal shelter as her two predecessors. Jersey Girl, a comical mixture of Yorkie and Chinese-crested powderpuff, was adopted from a local rescue group a few months later.

Not to be outdone by the memory of the senior boy dogs, these young girls swaggered as they survey the grounds once ruled by Max and Baylor. I wondered how their personalities and peculiarities would unfold. So far, neither has demonstrated an aptitude for soccer or eating snails, but they were fans of snack time, a good belly rub, and snarling at the mail carrier.

Dog tags jingled as Bandit and Jersey Girl romped around the yard, chasing after a bee or a butterfly. I closed my eyes and imagined that it was Max or Baylor barking at the sound of the neighbor's lawnmower.

In between keeping the water bowls full and the leashes ready for a walk, I learned a lot about commitment, trust, and love from a pair of pooches. Max and Baylor would be pleased that all those years of education wouldn't go to waste.

The Leader of the Pack

I stood in our backyard holding the chewed wires of what had been our automatic sprinkler system. Looking up at me was Bandit, our excited, twelve-pound rat terrier. Her docked tail wagging to beat the band, she was ready to chase a tennis ball or anything else I cared to throw her way. Her soulful eyes seemed to say: *"What? What's the problem?"* She didn't know how much trouble she (and I) were about to be in with my husband Nick.

This wasn't the first time our newly adopted pet had left her (teeth) mark on something of value. Bandit had only been a member of the family for a few weeks and already the damage was piling up. My son Seth's football jersey, the buttons on Nick's dress shirt and my pink cashmere slippers were the most recent casualties. We were learning fast that this eighteen-month-old pup secretly possessed a three-foot vertical leap. Nothing was safe.

At first, I was a nonbeliever. Clueless in the ways of this hunting breed, I thought that our possessions were secure if stored a couple feet off the floor. Goes to show how wrong a girl could be.

Proof positive came when Seth yelled to me from inside the garage. He'd just found Bandit curled atop his clean and neatly folded clothes, snoozing comfortably in the laundry basket on our pool table. She'd also nibbled the table's corners, but we haven't told Nick yet.

I hadn't been naïve enough to think that being Mom to Shawn, Jake, and Seth wouldn't include taking care of a pet or two. I knew I'd help with feeding, scooping, emptying, walking, and cleaning. But I never dreamed I'd be challenged like this.

Starting when Shawn was about four, we have loved dogs Buttons, Ozzie and Harriet, Butterscotch and Hopscotch, and cats Boots and Stripey. Our family menagerie included a series of hamsters known as Hamstie I, Hamstie II, and Shawn Claude von Hamstie; parakeets Larry, Phoenix, and Cheetah; and aquarium dwellers Wet and Feisty the Fish. None of these critters gave me any trouble—save a couple hamster breakouts, an occasional accident on the carpet, and a bird that didn't want to go back into her cage.

For the past ten years, our current pooches Max and Baylor have shared love, companionship, and an occasional dead opossum with us. We've watched their muzzles slowly turn gray and their lively gait slow to a saunter. Maybe that's why I thought it was a good idea to mix in a younger four-legged member to our household. Nick took a little more convincing.

I first spotted Bandit among row after row of animal faces peeking out from a local animal shelter ad. Some five hours later, we had a new member of the Fadden clan.

As part of the adoption process, we brought our two dogs to meet Bandit. They sniffed each other's backsides and wandered around the shelter's enclosure exploring new scents together. Max and Baylor paid little attention to their potential sister. They acted as though she seemed harmless enough.

Bandit was mellow for a couple of days after she was spayed. Her warm body nestled contently at my feet while I sat writing article after article. The vet's earlier warning was falling on deaf ears. "This breed is very smart," she had counseled. "They hunt and they are excellent watchdogs. But they need to be kept busy." Her advice to buy some puzzle toys left me puzzled. Why did this little pooch need interactive doggie toys to stay occupied?

Weeks later, as I stood among the wreckage— tattered Wiffle balls, chewed-up water bottles, and a lounge chair with arms that were reminiscent of Edward Scissorhands—I knew the answer.

Panicked, I went to see my niece Sara. Sara was the owner of Bella, the only other rat terrier I knew. Sympathetic to my quandary, Sara listened attentively, nodded knowingly, and then told me that my best chance for happiness with Bandit was to become a pack leader.

After I stopped laughing, I realized that she was serious. "You might not believe it, but you and your guys are her pack," she said, and then chuckled. "Get some dog training to learn the right way to discipline her. Bandit is a great dog, but she needs boundaries."

It took weeks of classes and several episodes of *The Dog Whisperer* before I learned pack-leader basics. A video game controller, a few T-shirts and a rosebush were sacrificed in exchange for my education.

Today, Bandit and I have a mutually satisfying relationship. In exchange for taking her on long walks, she won't jump on me or the couch. When she felt the urge to chew, she used one of her peanut-butter-and-kibble-filled toys instead of my new slippers.

And when Nick finally realized that the corners of his pool table were gnawed, Bandit and I agreed to deny knowing anything about it.

Branches on the Family Tree

I didn't like being the youngest. I'd complain about not being allowed to do the same things my brothers George and Paul, and my sister Sadye did. It wasn't fair that I had the earliest bedtime. It was no fun being the baby.

My older siblings viewed it differently. They thought I had the special spot in the family tree. Occasionally, they'd used another word (that also begins with sp) to describe the baby—spoiled.

That's because, thanks to their early trial-and-error efforts, my mom was a seasoned single parent by the time I was three. And that seasoning contributed to the person I am—out-going, creative and competitive—all traits associated with last-born children.

Oh yeah—and a little spoiled.

I'm a mom now. The birth order of my sons Shawn, Jake, and Seth doesn't affect how much I love them. But I have to confess that it's been a bit easier to parent my second child. And, like the comfort of using a broken-in baseball glove, Seth benefits from how Shawn and Jake softened the leather of my parenting skills.

In my mid-twenties when Shawn was born, I boiled everything—bottles, pacifiers, brushes, spoons, bowls. If something hadn't been thoroughly disinfected (at temperatures north of 180 degrees Fahrenheit), it didn't touch my baby's mouth.

I'd learned to lighten up some by the time Jake arrived. I was thirty and instead of boiling bottles, I listened when the pediatrician said it was okay to clean them in the dishwasher.

Seth came along four years later when many of my days were spent sitting in the Little League bleachers. During a brother's six-inning game, his bottle would hit the dirt a time or two. Not taking my eyes off the runner at third, I'd wipe it off on my jeans and, under a stream of soda poured from a snack bar cup, I'd rinse the nipple. I'm happy to report that Seth grew up quite healthy, in spite of an occasional trace of cola on his unsterilized milk bottle.

Some knowledge was borne out of practice. Some arrived out of self-preservation. With three kids and a job, I had to be a quick study. During that nine-year span and some 12,000 diaper changes later, many rough edges smoothed out. By the time I was waking up for Seth's midnight feedings, I'd worked my way up from rookie to expert to pro.

I'm still the same woman mothering this trio, but I haven't remained the same parent. Life doesn't work that way. My guys grew from infant to toddler to child to teen and I had to grow up alongside them. While figuring out the perfect temperature for a bottle of formula, and where to buy an athletic supporter, I was also learning which battles to wage and which ones to let go. Some of this insight emanated from sheer exhaustion, but I prefer to think of it as becoming wiser.

Before his brothers were born, Shawn enjoyed having his dad Nick and me to himself. But our undivided attention came with a price tag. While we frantically thumbed through volumes of parenting books, Shawn became the focus of our on-the-spot training. Like it or not, the first-born tested the waters for the siblings to follow. He crawled, toddled, walked, and then ran around the house as he experimented with how far to push the off-limits envelope.

The wise second child (who might become the middle child) took a spectator role. He watched the results and learned what's okay with Mommy and what buttons not to push.

Younger siblings don't have to train amateur parents. They are free to skate over ground that's already conquered and go on to create their own mischief. When they're big enough to play their own game of Childhood, the youngers skip some of the chutes the olders fell down. They quickly climb ladders that a big brother (or sister) propped up for them.

Occasionally our test case—I mean Shawn—complained about how easy his younger brothers had it.

"You never let me stay up that late when I was his age."

"I didn't get to _____ (fill in the blank) until I was _____ (two years older than whatever age Jake and/or Seth currently are)."

But I also overheard Shawn (and sometimes Jake) offer sage advice to younger brother, Seth: "Don't try it. Mom always finds out."

"You're better off just telling her the truth. She'll go easier on you."

Like their parents, Shawn, Jake and Seth continued to learn from experience.

And experience was the truest teacher, no matter what order your branch was added to the family tree.

Adventure in the Great Outdoors

I'm not the outdoorsy type. To me, roughing it is making mashed potatoes that don't come out of a box, or watching basic cable. My idea of a good time isn't a shopping trip to Patagonia, or any other sporting goods retailer. Rarely will you hear me use the phrase: "Pass the mosquito repellant."

Don't get me wrong; I love the great outdoors as much as the next gal. I was a cookie-selling Girl Scout a few decades ago, and I have proof—my needlecraft and storytelling badges. But nowadays, when it comes to choosing between roasting hot dogs around the campfire or washing my hair, you'll find me clutching a bottle of Pantene.

The fact that I'm not cut out to be nature-mom didn't matter to my sons. Shawn, Jake, and Seth had launched a month-long campaign, enlisting their dad Nick and me to go on a family camping trip. My boys—eager to use their sleeping bags somewhere other than a sleepover at a pal's house—wanted to trek into rustic untamed forests, nibble on trail mix and witness nature someplace other than on the Discovery Channel.

Unlike them, I'm quite content to experience nature at a distance; in books, at the zoo or on TV. My world is planned, controlled, and predictable. Mother Nature's world isn't. Camping would force me to step out of my comfort zone and display my tent-pitching, s'more-making and dunk-bag dishwashing skills—none of which I received a scouting badge for.

My sons' long-held dream of camping underneath the sky's canopy, far from the din of the city, was about to outweigh my apprehension. During dinner, I found myself face-to-face with a trio of would-be campers ready to venture into the wild. All of my excuses, pleas, and stall tactics landed on deaf ears.

Not wanting to travel too far to find nature, reluctantly I agreed on a site about thirty miles from home. The brochure for a nearby state park promised "...camping and hiking in an oak woodland forest, with a sprinkling of pines and lovely meadows with creeks."

I thought, *how bad could it be*? I envisioned filling my photo album with snapshots of five happy campers frolicking against a backdrop of sunshine and pristine scenery. Plans were made, gear purchased, reservations confirmed, and before we knew it, the Fad-five were embarking on their first camping expedition. Even though I wasn't the engine behind this wilderness weekend, I started looking forward to our June adventure—just me, my guys, and vistas of the countryside.

It took us longer to pack the van than to make the forty-minute drive to our site at Green Valley family camp. As I cautiously surveyed what would be our new home for the next three days, the guys started to unload our provisions. Seth, four years old at the time, happily carried his seldom-used sleeping bag to a clearing by a tree. Older brothers Jake, eight, and Shawn, twelve, followed behind, dragging the tent that claimed to be simple to set up.

Some ninety minutes later, our shelter was finally upright. The boys, waiting impatiently to try their luck at fishing, held their poles. With no time allowed to reflect on our tent success, Nick grabbed the tackle box. As we walked toward the lake, he began his speech on how to keep the lines untangled, despite the fact Nick knew he'd spend the remainder of the day unsnarling fishing line, baiting hooks, and demonstrating how to cast a reel. I could tell he'd given up hope of actually catching a fish that day.

In our rented rowboat in the middle of the lake, my four fishermen waited to make the catch of the day. I was busy taking photos when Shawn, looking at the numerous nimbus clouds gathering directly overhead, asked, "Mom, are those rain clouds?"

"There aren't any clouds over there," Jake said, pointing to the other end of the lake, just as the downpour let loose. I spotted a shelter on the nearby shore and shouted for our lead rower (Nick) to point the boat in that direction. Wet and fishless, we paddled for cover.

Our refuge? A newly installed outhouse. Well, any port (or port-a-potty) in a storm.

Back at the campsite, the news wasn't any better. While we rookie campers were catching our dinner, raccoons ransacked our unsecured coolers. Eight wieners, a few marshmallows and a pan of Jiffy Pop were spared.

That night, while laughing about rainy weather, unexpected dinner guests and the fish that got away, we feasted on blackened hot dogs, burned popcorn, and toasted marshmallows. Our dinner location had changed, but my family's character hadn't. During those three days, this camping family pulled together to overcome the elements. Our rudimentary scouting skills (and a hearty sense of humor) prevailed over capricious and unpredictable Mother Nature.

I wonder if it's too late to ask Mrs. Bright, my troop leader, to recommend me for an outdoor survival badge.

What I'll Do on My Summer Vacation

Summer is the best time for family vacations. Labor Day is a couple months away, daylight lingers, and no one has a book report due by Friday. My family sticks to this timetable, although it's not every twelve months we can afford to pack up the fivesome and caravan to a distant place. Big vacations are sprinkled in whenever we can swing them.

Even though we budget, often our travel plans put us in the red for a month or more. My husband and I don't mind. We know that the days are numbered until our three sons—Shawn, Jake, and Seth—realize they're too cool to hang out with Mom and Dad. We happily trade a healthy bank account for time together.

Past summers have been spent horseback riding in Kauai, boating on Lake Tahoe, or rafting down the American River in Sacramento. My sons have picnicked near the Golden Gate Bridge, took a cruise to the Bahamas, and trekked to Pittsburgh for a family reunion. We have photos of us in front of the Liberty Bell, the St. Louis Arch, and the Statue of Liberty.

But often, our school break is spent at home, devising our own (reasonably priced) entertainment. My fellas are content to cool off with a game of water Wiffle ball instead of dipping their toes in the ocean near Nassau. Boogie-boarding at the beach is an acceptable substitute for snorkeling in Cabo San Lucas.

In spite of financial reality, I'm not quite ready to do away with family vacations altogether. There are a few places I'd like to see with my sons before they're planning their own family vacations—Washington, DC and the Grand Canyon, to name two. But in between the major getaways, there's still plenty of ways to enjoy time together during the lazy, crazy, hazy days of summer. So, before the back-to-school bell rings, I'm hoping to:

-- Lick toasted marshmallows and melted chocolate off my fingers after a barbecue.

-- Really listen to the words of "America the Beautiful" when it's sung on the Fourth of July.

-- Mark on the den doorjamb how much taller Shawn, Jake, and Seth have grown since last summer.

-- Watch *Mary Poppins* (for what might be the 63rd time).

-- Make do-it-yourself Chipwiches. Use vanilla fudge ripple ice cream.

-- Avoid full-length mirrors while wearing my one-piece "slimsuit."

-- Score big-time in a water balloon fight.

-- Hug my sons every chance I get.

-- Hit a Wiffle ball over our backyard fence for a home run.

-- Use a lot of SPF 30.

-- Mix up bowls of Candy Apple Salad (equal parts: Granny Smith apples, Snickers, and Cool Whip).

-- Take in an afternoon Padres' game. Sing "God Bless America" and "Take Me Out to the Ballgame."

-- Buy some peanuts and Cracker Jack.

-- Keep quiet when the boys use all of my ice cube trays to make strawberry Kool-Aid-flavored pops.

-- Buy a new sun hat.

-- Win a game of *Wizard of Oz Monopoly* – or get sleepy trying.

-- See the summer blockbuster movies. Crunch the buttery theatre popcorn.

-- Recall the fun I had as a little girl, catching lightning bugs after dark in southwestern Pennsylvania.

-- Smile at the memory of my mom's voice telling me to let them go.

-- Tempt fate and try my luck on the Slip 'n Slide.

-- Avoid travel brochures touting romantic getaways to Rome, Paris, or Athens.

-- Eat cotton candy and grilled corn-on-the-cob at the fair.

-- Dust off our telescope and be amazed at the jewels found in the night sky.

-- Duck when my youngest son targets me with his new squirt gun. Catch him off guard with my super soaker.

-- Take lots of pictures. Get prints made before Halloween.

-- Ignore that Y-shaped tan line my feet get after wearing sandals.

-- Taste the tomatoes, zucchini, and green peppers Nick grew in our backyard garden.

-- Shun the back-to-school shopping ads that come out in early July.

-- Enjoy the extra hours of sunlight.

-- Curl up on my patio glider and read, read, read.

-- Hum along with Carly Simon and be reminded that these are the good old days.

Brothers, Sisters, and Other Hazards of Growing Up

When I close my eyes, I can see them. Spades, diamonds, clubs, and hearts streaming through the air. I had forgotten about that day until recently, after winning a game of computer solitaire. It took a few attempts before my reward—a parade of aces, jacks, kings, and queens—cascaded across my screen. Their cavalier celebration reminded me of another time, though, when I was about five and my reaction to flying playing cards was very different.

It happened after my friends Amy and Patti were called home. We'd been playing Barbies, but now I was bored. That made me a prime target for getting tricked by a couple of smart-alecky teenagers (aka my big brothers George and Paul), who didn't want to waste their time entertaining their baby sister.

After pestering them to play, they suggested a game I'd never heard of before: 52 Pick-Up. "You sure you want to play, Claire?" George asked, shuffling the cards in his hand. I nodded excitedly. Getting to do something with my brothers was a big deal. Usually they were too busy hanging out with friends or on their way to basketball practice to make time for me.

Seconds later, I watched the deck of fifty-two playing cards fan out through the air and land scattered across the living room floor. My brown eyes filled with tears as both brothers, laughing hysterically, shouted: "Pick up! Pick up!"

"You said you wanted to play," Paul reminded me, nodding to George, proud that they had fooled a kindergartner. But even at my young age, I was smart enough to turn on the little sister tears. Before I knew it, they were helping me clean up and we were on our way to Pulio's corner drugstore for chocolate ice cream cones.

Getting teased, tricked, and bothered by older siblings pretty much comes with the territory. But there is an upside to being the youngest of the family. By the time my parents brought me home from the hospital, my big sister Sadye and my brothers had already cleared the path. Being normal kids, they'd done just about everything kids can do to their parents long before I'd ever thought of it.

Psychologists tout the need for siblings, too. Their reasoning: siblings entertain each other and teach each other how to work together. "If you want to be a real parent," my long-time friend Teresa says, "you have to have at least two kids. Otherwise when something breaks, it's too easy to figure out who did it."

Providing our firstborn with a sibling (or two) to blame stuff on was a shaky reason to have more than one child. Nevertheless, over an eight-year span, my husband Nick and I added three branches to our family tree.

Our sons have their own opinions of our family's size. In jest (we think), Shawn questioned why we had more kids. He claimed that things were just fine as an only child when he got all the attention, all the toys, and no one to have to share them with. Seth, the youngest, was convinced that the oldest kid had it the best—Shawn never had to wear hand-me-downs, got to stay up later, and did everything first. Jake, the middle child…well, you know. He's the middle child.

The trio, spaced about four years apart, are a volatile combination of best friends and worthy adversaries.

They joined forces early in life, pursuing a quest to keep their parents off balance. The result of their not-so-secret pact finds Nick and me engaged in an unending game of *Whodunit?*

"Who put the wet towel on the rug?"

"Who left an empty toilet paper roll?"

"Who wore my baseball cap and didn't return it?

Fights in the back seat, name-calling, and protests of "he punched me," "he threw Cheetos at me," or "he broke my iPod," are familiar lyrics blaring through the soundtrack of our bustling family life. Occasionally, when the noise reverberates to a new level, Nick and I are tempted to rethink our decision. But then reality weighs in. We take a deep breath and bask in the pride we feel for the relationships they have cultivated.

Shawn was the voice of experience to his younger brothers. Jake got to have a big brother and be one, too. And Seth learned from the successes and frustrations of his older siblings.

As far as I can tell, no one's been tricked into a game of 52 Pick-Up. These guys manufactured their own brand of agitating, taunting, pestering, and brotherly love. Their methods have changed, but the Number One Sibling Rule—*be as annoying as possible to each other*—remains intact. Wiffle ball games which pitted brother against brother, sock fights in the dark, and weekend games of cutthroat *Monopoly* are their current devices of choice.

Watching from the sidelines, Nick and I stayed out of the crossfire. From our position, we refereed this trio's squabbles, kept the pantry stocked with ammunition, and attempted to figure out who left the empty milk carton in the fridge.

It's Why You Play the Game That Counts

I was sipping my second cup of creamer-laced coffee when I learned that classic board games were "getting a speed boost." The article in the business section of the daily paper grabbed my attention. It touted marketers who were reinventing our best-loved pastimes to accommodate busier lives and shorter attention spans. These newly-tailored versions of old-time favorites will now only take twenty minutes to play.

I guess it was just a matter of time before family game night took the express route.

Living with a group of guys who need twenty minutes just to decide which game to play made it hard to imagine this acceleration. These new versions suggested that I'd concede defeat to any one of my three sons in about the same amount of time it took to microwave a meatloaf dinner. Up until now, the only game we played that fast was *Perfection* and that's because there's a sixty-second timer built in.

It's not new that families today were moving at the speed of life. I'm referring to jam-packed schedules, not the board game. Even so, when my sons were little (under five years old), my husband Nick and I made time to sit cross-legged on the family room floor and try our luck at *Candy Land* (*Chutes and Ladders, Memory, Hi Ho! Cherry-O*, or whatever game caught their interest that week).

This usually meant that we'd end up on the losing side of these encounters, often on purpose. I learned early on that, if I won, it automatically signaled that I'd be challenged to another game, where I was guaranteed to come in last. A single game could easily evolve into the best-of-seven series for *Candy Land* supremacy and household bragging rights.

A typical scenario went something like this: After a preschool-age Shawn (or Jake or Seth) "randomly" shuffled the cards and placed them on the board, Shawn (or Jake or Seth) would pull the Queen Frostine card and be transported to mere spaces away from certain victory. This was a long-standing family mystery that could only be matched by my uncanny ability to pick the Plumpy card and be banished to the space marked with a plum at the start of the *Candy Land* game board.

Defeat was certain. Their eyes held a twinkle of glee at their imminent triumph as I hammed up my disappointment at being sent back to the beginning.

These early years of playing games designed for the under-seven set passed quickly. During this wonderful opportunity, my boys learned how to count their moves correctly, not fight over the green gingerbread marker, play fair, and be a good loser. Years later, I realized that they had become competent adversaries, no longer needing a stacked deck to insure a victory. The tables had turned and I often found myself trying my best just to make a good showing. The roles of teacher and student switched and I was hearing my words of comfort coming out of their mouths. "Don't worry, Mom. You'll win next time. Don't give up. Just keep trying."

My next strategy was to engage my sons in games where I thought I had an edge. However, I didn't have much success mustering up enthusiasm for a rousing game of hopscotch. Everyone claimed to be too busy or too tired to be lured into a heated round of jacks and I swear that someone—probably Nick—hid my *Mystery Date* game. I guess they didn't like the deck stacked in my favor. But just mention *Cranium, Scattergories,* or the sports version of *Scene It?* and suddenly, holes in their schedules magically opened up.

As they got older, my sons' interest in playing games with our family stayed constant. Those lazy afternoons filled with *Monopoly, Double Trouble* or *Clue* transformed into *Catch Phrase, Balderdash* or an evening of *Guitar Hero*, a music video game where they'd challenge me to play "Free Bird" on the hard setting. The game selection evolved and there might not be an actual board involved anymore, but we still played. Our game nights have expanded to include their circle of friends. We loved sharing the laughter, the joys of competition, and just being together. No one was concerned about how long it took.

I'm not convinced that faster is better. There's still a place for the luxury of the steady, slow pace of playing games. These new twists on the classics that revved up the time it took to finish might be fixing something that wasn't really broken. There's always tomorrow. If bedtime showed up before our game of *Monopoly* is done, we just move it—board and all—to the top of our seldom-used dining room table.

Tonight, if I'm lucky, the TV, the computer, and the video game system will get turned off. My four guys and I will replace those amusements with a spirited discussion of who wants to be the race car, the dog, the top hat, or the wheelbarrow. Me, I'm always the thimble.

Choosing our playing pieces for *Monopoly*...now *that's* something we can finish in twenty minutes or less.

The Refrigerator Door

Most people think that the primary purpose of my refrigerator door is to keep the food inside cold—the lettuce crisp, the milk fresh.

They are wrong.

My fridge door isn't just protecting ice cream from melting. It's really an appliance-sized art gallery, showcasing my family's personality.

It's not uncommon to see my fridge blanketed with shopping lists, old report cards, and pizza coupons that expired yesterday. Sure, there's the occasional art project— a Popsicle stick-laden magnet that names me *World's Best Mom,* penned in a six-year-old's best handwriting.

The white panels of my refrigerator door survived many stages of this growing family. Right now there is a photo of my oldest son Shawn and his pal Mike, standing proudly alongside their catch of the day. There's a photo of Jake, too. He's walking across the football field with three other players. All four are team captains for the high school game. Our youngest son Seth is pictured with his best pals, our dogs Max and Baylor.

In days past, I would post reminders: *The letter of the week is T.* (A notice to start looking for twenty things that began with the letter T before Monday morning.) Or *Snack Day is Saturday.* Our fridge doubles as a gigantic magnetic letter board, where all three boys moved around colorful letters in their early attempts to learn the alphabet.

Through winning and losing seasons, both Pirates' and Steelers' schedules were displayed. Right now we have a *Save the Date* note, reminding us of a nephew's upcoming wedding. Magnets like my *I Love Lucy* one and Nick's *100% Irish* shamrock hold miscellaneous notes, reminders, and prayers. The door is the place to hang school awards, showcase newspaper clippings of athletic and scholastic success, and cute photos of precious additions to our family.

Gaining refrigerator space means you've arrived. This is big. There's only so much room, so the keeper of this oversized, noisy marquee (aka *me*) must be selective. That's when the trouble begins—what to keep and what to move to the scrapbook pile or the trash heap. It takes a mixture of tact and ruthlessness to know when a "door item" has run its course.

How do I make these tough decisions? Well, if papers fall to the floor every time I close my refrigerator door, I ask these questions. They guide me in my quest to part with some of these memories.

Is the clipping yellowed or from another decade?

Is the preschooler whose finger-painting is hanging on my fridge now submitting applications to colleges?

Do I remember why I put that on the fridge in the first place? Do I know which kid supplied it?

Will anybody notice if I remove it?

Yes, being the keeper of the refrigerator door is a big job. But someone's got to do it. And who better than us moms? That way we can be certain that what we want stays on the door. Like my ladybug magnet given to me by my niece, Frances. It has center stage on our Amana.

Among the family's calendar, soccer announcements, and works of art, sandwiched between the pizza coupons and dental reminders, beats the heart of my family. Each time I reach for the milk, or take out the lunchmeat, I'm faced with our running news banner. It's always on, streaming through whatever we're doing.

This haphazard window into my family's life keeps me focused on how quickly time passes.

Mom's Pool Hall

Friends Welcome. Cars Prohibited.

I'm in awe of my neighbors. They park their cars inside their garages.

I realize that this isn't a minor miracle and I shouldn't indulge in covered-parking envy. My neighbors aren't doing anything worth marveling at. But every day they accomplish a feat that continues to elude me.

We bought our 1968-built house nearly two decades ago. The realtor's multiple listing offered it as a three-bedroom, two-bath, with a fireplace, a family room and, of course, a two-car garage. All standard stuff.

Since we signed the escrow papers, we have slept in the bedrooms, we have showered in the bathrooms, we have watched TV in the family room, and yes, there have been fires in the fireplace. On the other hand, I'm sorry to say that nothing gas-powered, minus the lawnmower, has been stored in the garage since Ronald Reagan was president. The last vehicle in there was a battery-operated ride-on Jeep that my son Shawn rode when he was seven.

Perhaps the previous owners had this figured out. Maybe they were extravagant enough to station not one, but two cars inside the garage. We never talked about it, so I really don't know. But I frequently imagined how it could be.

Fantasy: I'm driving home from work. It's raining. My car is full of healthy fruits and vegetables I purchased to replenish my barren cupboards. I pull into my driveway, push the button and watch in awe as my sectioned garage door rolls up. I drive into my garage and park. Not a drop of rainwater touches my hair or the twenty-three plastic-handled bags of groceries I effortlessly maneuver into the kitchen.

Reality: After a long day at work and stopping at the market for a pre-cooked chicken and a box of ready-in-minutes au gratin potatoes, I park on the street. It's pouring. I make two trips to the car to transport my meager bags, purse, and briefcase from vehicle to kitchen. In less than 6.3 seconds, I resemble a woman who's taken a wrong turn at the waterpark and ended up going down Paradise Plunge headfirst.

What happened to that two-car garage we bought all those years ago? It has been transformed into a billiard hall/weight room/storage center. And even the pool table multitasks, doubling as a surface for folding laundry. Oh, that's right, our garage is a laundry room/gift-wrapping center, too. There should be a sign posted: No cars allowed!

While I longed for a place to put everything—including my car—my sons and their dad promoted a place to have fun. Over the years I've relinquished the hope that these two goals can peacefully coexist in a 600-square-foot garage. I've come to accept this impromptu, cement-slabbed game room. It was the site of many billiard happenings, Friday night gatherings, and spur-of-the-moment get-togethers.

It's even attracted the media. Not long ago, our gray felt-covered table made it on the evening news.

For some moms, this might be a predicament—comfort and convenience versus accommodating a bunch of guys. But as a reasonable and outnumbered woman, I asked myself what's really important: enjoying the luxury of parking my seven-year-old minivan in a covered facility or providing a place for my sons and their friends to play.

From the time our boys were young—even before we were blessed with all three—my husband and I knew we wanted to be the "Kool-Aid house." You know, the place where the neighborhood kids hung out. We wanted to be the spot where all the kids felt welcome, long before we ever thought about buying a pool table. With somewhat mixed emotions, I can report that this naïve dream has come true. Not too much Kool-Aid is being served, but my soda and bottled water bills continued to increase as Shawn's, Jake's, and Seth's friends felt more and more comfortable hanging out here.

So as you can imagine, I'm not putting my car in what's become the Fadden Family Pool Hall. In fact, there are days that I can't even park in the driveway—that's frequently converted into a basketball court. So what if I have to settle for a spot halfway up the cul-de-sac and haul my twenty-three reusable grocery bags?

I now insist that these pool-playing, basket-shooting teens call "time out" to assist this little old lady with her packages. There's always lots of hands to help…as long as I'm willing to wait until they're in between shots.

The Nearness of Neighbors

I'm watching a steady stream of Wiffle balls cascade over my backyard fence. My neighbors, Carol and Ernie, toss them back about once a week.

They've been doing this for a lot of years and it's one of the reasons why I live on this quiet cul-de-sac in Chula Vista. Twelve houses make up the horseshoe-shaped street nicknamed *The Court*. Really wonderful people live here. People I can call on to borrow a cup of sugar, two eggs, or last week's coupon section from the Sunday newspaper. Because of the busyness of the workweek, it's rare to see each other unless it's a quick wave while driving by. Still, I know that any time I'm in need, I have my choice of good Samaritans willing to loan a cooler, move a couch, or house-sit. Of course, Nick and I are happy to return the favor, whether with a stick of margarine, loaning lawn clippers, or finding a spot in our garage to hide a bike until Christmas.

Even though we may go weeks without real conversation, I know I can count on this group of men, women, and kids. But like any quality relationship, you must work at it. And we do that during our occasional, impromptu grocery-store meetings.

Sure, I know what you're thinking. Most neighbors exchange hellos over the fence or chat while they pull weeds in their front yards. Somehow those tried-and-true methods don't work for our gang. Rarely do I even see a neighbor when I pick up the morning paper off the driveway. But if I want to connect with any of them, all I need to do is run out of hamburger buns for dinner and dash to the store for a minute. With my hair looking like it was styled by Edward Scissorhands, you can bet I'll see every neighbor and friend from blocks around.

The scenario repeated itself so often that, now whenever I go out of the house, even if it's just to pick up a carton of milk, I comb my hair, check my blouse for any noticeable stains and put on some lipstick. I don't want to frighten someone today who might be helping me move a dresser tomorrow.

Our grocery store meetings materialize just about anywhere: the cereal aisle, near the meat section, or at the bakery counter. It takes just a couple minutes to catch up and reconnect. "What teacher does David have this year?" "Did Katie pass her driving test?" "Who painted your house?" Answers to these quick questions between the butter and the bacon are all we need to keep our alliances flourishing.

I'm grateful for this food-centered meeting place. Otherwise, I might go for months without actual conversations with people who help out in a moment's notice. Unlike my best friend who now lives in Riverside, these folks are seconds away. They offer a safe place to store an extra house key in case one of my sons forgets his. And they can be counted on to have the tool Nick needs to fix the sink. Where else can I go with three gallons of ice cream when my freezer breaks? Riverside's a bit far to drive with my *chocolate chip cookie dough* melting.

A few years ago, when our family grew from three to four to five, Nick and I considered moving from our cozy three-bedroom house. Our quest for more room found us reading the real estate ads and contemplating a newer area. Of course the papers listed the square footage and number of bedrooms. We'd have a great room, walk-in closets, a whirlpool bathtub. But it's the info that wasn't listed that I was interested in. I wanted to know: Would the lady across the street let me borrow her jigsaw puzzles? How did the would-be neighbors on my right feel about waves of Wiffle balls flying over their fence? Who'd chase down our dogs, Max and Baylor, if they got out? Questions no realtor could answer.

Homes are more than stucco and tile, carpentry and plumbing, two-car garages and sprinkler systems. That's what you see on the outside, but that's not what keeps the Faddens living on this cul-de-sac in a somewhat remodeled home. It's the round-the-clock hospitality we share with the people living inside the homes near ours. The richness of our neighborhood isn't found in the rose bushes, jacaranda trees, and manicured lawns. They look great, but it's the people I treasure.

I'm sure we would have found terrific folks in the new subdivision, but thanks to room additions, we'll never find out.

So, as we start another school year on *The Court*, I'm happy to say that Robin lets me borrow her puzzles. Anne has our extra house key. Ernie and Carol still return the Wiffle balls that found their way over the fence, and the Ballard twins call about once a month to say that Max and Baylor got out again, "but don't worry, we have them."

As for Nick and me, we're still hanging our clothes in a regular-sized closet, bathing in a standard tub and watching TV in our converted family room. And we think that's just great.

A Girl, Four Guys, & Football

Around my house I'm outnumbered. I'm pink in a world of blue. Three sons, one husband. Even the two dogs, Max and Baylor, are male. When everyone else stands up, I'm sitting down. I'm the only girl in a house full of guys, and it's lonely. No one to show new shoes to. No one to care about a bra sale at Kohl's. No one to share clothes with.

So how does a lone girl even the playing field when she lives with four guys? By picking up her game. Her football game, that is.

With my days bombarded with ESPN—the TV station and the magazine—you learn quickly how to be in with the in-crowd. And with this crowd, you have to know football. That's why I now throw words like *depth-chart* and *free safety* around with apparent abandon. I'm fitting in and I hope that soon I'll learn what they mean. *Bye week, wide receiver and Wing T* are terms I've come to know. I can discuss a team's defense or chances for a wild card bid as easily as I can share my recipe for cheeseburger soup.

The real test of fitting in with my guys comes in the mastery of the Fadden Football Pool, known around here as the FFP. Each week, the five of us try our hand at predicting the correct outcome of the week's football match-ups.

It's a simple contest with simple rules: Someone, usually Nick, cuts out the odds board from the sports page of the daily paper and tapes it to the official FFP clipboard. The rest of us take turns writing down our predictions on the official FFP tally sheet.

Suitable for bragging rights, the sheet features a spot to pay homage to last week's winner. Typically, this is my youngest son, Seth. He tends to pick all the favorites.

We've enjoyed this light-hearted family rivalry for twenty seasons. Starting in late August through the January playoffs—even if a son is away at college and has to phone in his choices, or someone has the flu—one thing can be counted on; the FFP. With player names like Daddray, MegaMom, SonicShawn, Jakeman and $ethMoney, the gloves are off each week to have your moniker posted as the winner. Come game time, any one of us can be found holding the clipboard where the prediction sheet is secured. In the other hand is a yellow marker, ready to highlight the names of the winning teams.

Here we've found a common ground—girl and boy alike. To win the FFP, it takes the perfect blend of football smarts, a sense of humor, and a whole lotta luck. It doesn't matter if your cologne is *Wind Song* or *Aramis,* to champion the FFP takes skill that transcends gender.

With thirty-two teams and sixteen match-ups most weeks, the total number of wins possible varied during the season. There have been weeks when I've been crowned champion before the Monday Night Football coin toss. There have also been times when my win total was less than my shoe size. The outcome every week is different and whomever is victorious gloats over the rest of us.

Each Sunday, my family gathered in front of the big screen to watch the players, listen to the commentators, and make a few comments of their own. As I claimed my seat in the blue recliner, water bottle in one hand and a bag of Scoops tortilla chips in the other, I hoped that it will be my name emblazoned as the week's winner. But winning wasn't what matters. I've already won because of the camaraderie I shared with my husband and my sons. They didn't want to spend time scrapbooking with me. My requests to go to afternoon tea have fallen on deaf ears. No takers to join me for a pedicure.

But just mention the football pool and we chat up a storm. Not knowing if Green Bay's punter pulled his groin muscle or Atlanta's quarterback is out for the week, I still managed to fake conversation with the best of 'em. Just because I'm outnumbered doesn't mean I have to be outsmarted.

Nike turf or natural grass, we've found a common ground and it's green with white lines. Just perfect for a pink girl in a blue world.

MOTHERHOOD MOMENTS

Music to My Ears

One random weeknight, my youngest son Seth and I were alone for dinner. The rest of the family had other plans for their evening meal, and rather than cook for just two, I suggested eating out. My 14-year-old easily agreed.

The hard part was deciding on where. Seth likes burgers. Me, I'm a salad eater. We compromised and went to Fuddruckers where we both could have what we wanted. Salad-eater mom also likes chocolate milkshakes. So does hamburger teen. Luckily, they have those, too.

The décor was casual and haphazard. On our way to our table, we passed a cluster of kids gathered around the electronic games. A clothesline was suspended across the center of the dining room, sporting a pair of boxers and a camisole secured by wooden clothespins. A popular spot with young families, the eatery is frequently the site of end-of-the-season team parties. This mom and son fit right in.

We weren't in a video-game-playing mood, so we spent our pre-eating time surveying the restaurant. Seth spotted the Rolling Stones booth dotted with framed photos of the band. Out of place was a solo picture of the Beatles that belonged on the wall of the booth across the way. My son, who fancied himself as a bit of a classic rock fan, can rattle off song titles made popular by each group. He loved the photo salute to both bands, as well as the booth dedicated to The King. Posters of Frank Sinatra and Marilyn Monroe graced the walls. Wayward hubcaps, battered suitcases, baseball pennants, and wooden fruit crates complemented the blast to the past.

Attached to the wall above the table Seth and I were seated, eagerly awaiting our chocolate shakes, was more of the same. Our section had an addition to the design scheme, though; three flat black discs mounted to the wall. They each had a hole in the middle about the size of a JFK half-dollar.

Immediately recognizable to me; not so much to my iPod-toting son.

Being a teenage seeker of knowledge, he was curious about these objects from another time. "Is that how you listened to music when you were my age?" he asked.

Born more than a decade after music CDs became popular, Seth had no reason to know about 45s, 78s, or LPs. Cassettes and 8-tracks are antiquated to him as well. He finds them about as useful as black-and-white TV.

These three small platters took me back to when I collected such items. I wondered if any of the titles were ones I owned in my youth: "I Think I Love You" (The Partridge Family); "Build Me Up Buttercup" (The Foundations); or "Tears of a Clown" (Smokey Robinson and the Miracles). But they weren't. They were tunes I'd never heard of.

"Those are called 45s," I explained to my son, already wondering where his dinner was, "because they were played at 45 rpm, revolutions per minute. We also called them singles," I added. Sensing that he might be interested, I ventured on. "People owned record players. We'd meet at a friend's house, bring stacks of records and take turns playing our favorite songs." He nodded, but I could see his eyes begin to glaze over. I really lost him when I started chatting about the A and B sides. "The hit song was on the A side. The B side was a song you'd never heard before," I said, reaching for our newly arrived shakes.

In our house, Seth was the tech rep. If you needed to program a ring to your cell phone, add software on your computer or burn a CD, he's the go-to guy. It felt odd telling him about the beginnings of music technology (especially when the look on his face made me feel like I was lecturing from firsthand experience about events occurring in the Stone Age).

He couldn't imagine that something the size of an individual pan pizza could transmit music. They were too big to fit into a CD player. There was no disc drive in the computer where they would go.

I struggled with the comparison. His iPod, about the size of my palm, can hold one thousand tunes. Singles held two—tops. If Seth tried to amass as many songs in this outmoded format as his MP3 player can hold, he'd need 500 of them. Stacking about sixteen records per inch, the tower would reach past his shoulders. Forget about transporting that column of black vinyl and a record player to the beach. Also hard to take them along for an afternoon jog.

As he took his last bite of burger and finished it off with a couple fries, he smiled at me. "I'm glad things changed. It's so much better to listen to music this way." He pointed to the set of earbuds he had dangling around his neck.

I agreed. Mom and son could both enjoy "Satisfaction," "Jailhouse Rock," or "Let It Be." They sounded just as good now as they did when I was fourteen, and they're just a push-button away.

Mom! You're Embarrassing Me!

Most people think teenagers worry about getting a date to the prom, scoring a goal in soccer, or passing calculus. Not true. What keeps teens up at night is wondering when the next Mom-sponsored embarrassing moment will arrive. It's easy to be a source of chagrin to my kids.

In the right setting, everything I do—including breathing the same air—can be considered embarrassing. Simple reminders about taking a jacket when it's cold, asking what the movie is rated, or the name of a new girlfriend can qualify for sincere eye-rolls.

Interestingly, the bar for embarrassment rises in direct proportion to how old your children are. Quality humiliating moments get further apart as your children age. Even if you can't embarrass your teens as often, there are many gentle gems of playful teasing waiting to be unearthed.

I mastered this clandestine art under one of the best—my mom. She didn't try to annoy me on purpose, you understand. She was a rascal by nature—a girl kept after school for dipping another student's braid in the inkwell.

Before I was old enough to drive, Mom was my chauffeur—Girl Scout meetings, drama class, violin lessons. As a gag, she'd slide in behind the steering wheel and scoot her five-feet-one frame down to where she could scarcely see over the dashboard. Then we'd tool down the main drag. She saw other folks "low-driving" and she wanted to do it, too.

Mom would stay that way for several blocks while I prayed no one I knew would pull up alongside her Ford Falcon and see me riding shotgun. I don't remember where we were going on many of those taxi rides, but my mind's eye vividly sees the mischievous twinkle in Mom's eyes. It was years before I realized she was filling those random childhood moments with warmth, spontaneity, and love.

The next monumental embarrassment landed a few years later. I was still living at home and excited about a first date with a guy named Nick. He took me for a beachy picnic in Coronado, a reasonably-priced outing for a young man on a budget, but the March afternoon turned windy and cold. It was early afternoon when he brought me home. I asked him in and we decided to play cards. Within moments, Mom had pulled up a dining room chair and started shuffling. I felt my cheeks redden, but before I could signal her to ams-scray, they were laughing and sharing poker-playing tips. Needless to say, a year later when he proposed, I said yes, not sure which one of us he fell in love with first.

You can't wholly orchestrate these kinds of awkward moments. I believe the lasting ones come spontaneously, without planning, preparation, or forethought. Over time, I've discovered what Mom knew all along—what's mortifying at thirteen transforms into a magical memory by the time you're thirty-three.

Someday, my three sons—Shawn, Jake and Seth—will appreciate the playful seeds of teasing, antics, and practical jokes I've planted along their paths. I hope they cultivate an awareness of joyful simplicity, an easygoing sense of humor, and a keen ability to laugh at themselves.

If you're new at this gentle-embarrassment game, reflect on the impromptu things your parents said and did that sent you ducking for cover. I'm happy to share a few ideas that have worked in my world. Happy memory-making!

Top 10 Ways to Embarrass Your Kids without Really Trying

10. Kiss him in public.

9. Wipe off the lipstick smudge from your kiss with a tissue wetted with your saliva.

8. Pick her up from school wearing your purple and orange Zumba outfit.

7. Greet her new boyfriend with a handshake and a hearty "Hi, Jason," because you forgot this fellow's name is Damon. (My mom did this, but the actual names—Bill and Nick—have been changed to preserve peace in my home.)

6. Learn the lyrics to Wyclef Jean's "Historia" and sing along on carpool day.

5. Be the first couple on the dance floor at every wedding reception. For extra fun, lead the guests in the macarena or the electric slide.

4. Volunteer as the team mom*. If someone's beaten you to that coveted role, become the most enthusiastic fan in the bleachers. (*Room mom, field trip chaperone, cheer mom qualify.)

3. Use a coupon to pay for dinner, sneakers, movies—oh, just about anything.

2. Friend him on Facebook. Learn how to text. Have more followers than he does on Twitter.

1. Low-drive down Main Street. Trust me, you'll both laugh about this someday.

Look, Son, No Hands

With a controller in one hand and a spindly book of directions in the other, I'd spent the better part of Saturday morning failing to unlock the secrets of motion-controlled video games. Touted as a great way to infuse aerobic exercise into our daily routine, I'd bought the system for my husband Nick's birthday so we could bowl, river-raft, or score a goal in the comfort of our home.

I pushed every button and highlighted every TV screen option. No luck. Nick tried to help, but we both grew up in the generation that thought Pong and Space Invaders were futuristic. As I coached, Nick stood in front of the system's motion-detector, resembling an amateur airman flagging down planes. He swung his right arm up, then his left arm out. He might have gotten a bit of a workout, but none of his gyrations got the console to perform.

As a last resort, we hollered upstairs for our son Seth's help. Several minutes later, he joined us in the family room and surveyed the situation. "You and Dad are going to have to learn how to operate these things by yourselves. I'm not going to live here forever, you know." He shrugged, then left to play basketball with his friends.

"What do we do now?" my mate asked, keenly aware we'd become techno-dependent on the solo teen in the house. Unlike his boomer parents, our Generation "Z"er (aka the Net Generation) take technology for granted. Seth grew up alongside cell phones, touch screens, and YouTube. He and his pals never loaded a roll of film into a camera.

Nick and I aren't computer-helpless but in Seth's eyes, perhaps we were hopeless. Sure, it might take a few attempts before I downloaded a ringtone. And just last week I helped Nick activate a sports alert app on his smartphone. We've programmed the DVR, updated our Netflix queue, and paid bills online, so why did this rejection leave us feeling like we were being tough-loved into the 21st century?

I thought parents gave the self-reliance lecture, encouraging their children to spread their wings and fly. When had the tables turned? Somewhere during his childhood, the "teach a man to fish" mantra we espoused stuck. Now Nick and I were faced with a new truth: Seth would no longer be our shortcut to unravel electronic enigmas, like why my text message keyboard switched to Japanese. After years of generously serving as our personal tech support, our youngest was yanking the training wheels off our virtual bike and forcing us to pedal ourselves into the digital revolution.

I'm sure it hurt his heart to nix us from his unlimited knowledge of webcams and portable flash drives. But it was for our own good. Perhaps he saw a future filled with hapless, dependent parents relying on him for lifelong tech support. It was time he let us go, so we could choose our own gamertags.

I re-read the Quick Setup Guide, more committed than ever to getting the game to work. *I'll show him,* I thought. I couldn't let any of our three children think they were the products of techno-newbies from the generation responsible for platform shoes, audiocassettes, and Shake-a-Puddin'. No integrated circuit would defeat these two college-educated adults.

Reality set in forty-five minutes later, when Nick picked up the house phone, dialed customer support and handed me the receiver. The technician—probably close to Seth's age—didn't make a single "tsk" sound, and even though I couldn't see him, I'm pretty sure there weren't any eye-rolls on the other end of the line. In fact, once the system was operating, he asked what else he could help with. I fought the urge to have him walk me through setting up a wireless computer network.

Seth popped into the family room a few hours later and grinned. He put his hands on his hips and nodded at the TV screen. "I knew you could do it," he said, and then positioned himself to beat us in several games of volleyball.

Although he jettisoned his folks on the computer high seas, I'm not one to hold a grudge. In years to come, Seth can count on me for help when a college roommate leaves an ink pen in the washing machine, dying his laundry cornflower blue. I'll generously offer my advice on how to unstick a garbage disposal and where to find the best deal on paper plates. I'll even share my popular cheesy-meatloaf recipe.

Only now, when he calls, I won't be so eager to answer on the first ring.

Dad's A Catch!

Earlier today—five a.m., to be exact—I found myself sitting at our kitchen table, both hands curled around a lukewarm mug of coffee. My sons Shawn, Jake, and Seth, had just left with their dad for a day of deep-sea fishing. For some crazy reason, I felt the need to get up early and see them off.

My quartet of fellas—donning jackets, gloves, and baseball hats and carrying a tackle box full of fishhooks—looked somewhere between sleepy and joyful as they walked out the front door. An ocean adventure on the horizon.

A day on the high seas is not my idea of a great time. The closest I'm willing to get to a body of water is a spa pedicure, like the one I indulged in this afternoon. Thankfully, none of my hobbies involve waking up before the sun rises, taking seasick pills, or inhaling the scent of fresh mackerel.

The same isn't true for men; or at least, not my four. They have no aversion to stinky, gory, or dangerous. Securing a slimy worm on a hook is no big deal. My husband can live blissfully with bits of dirt captured under his fingernails, and never worry about breaking one of them during a basketball game of HORSE. He searches for TV shows about shark attacks, dirty jobs, and battles between Sparta and Athens. Threadbare T-shirts, hole-y socks, jeans that look like they were just shot out of a wrinkle gun—all part of the male bravado.

Dads like my husband are heralded for teaching kids useful stuff, like how to hit a Wiffle ball off a tee, draw to an inside straight, or burp "Yankee Doodle." Athletic supporters, nine irons, and cleats aren't a mystery. Nick has taught our trio how to tie a Windsor knot, use an electric shaver, and repair a leaky spigot. Clutching a pipe wrench, this handy dad tutored his sons on the merits of "righty-tighty, lefty-loose-y."

I'm glad to be the contrast to Nick's daddyhood. This mom has introduced her kids to black-and-white TV sitcoms, Motown, and chocolate chip cookie dough. As they grew, I imparted a mixture of practical (check for TP before you sit down), emotional (laugh some everyday) and spiritual (what goes around, comes around) wisdom. Because of me, my sons can sew on a button, shop for the best price on a box of cereal, and avoid burning their grilled-cheese sandwiches.

I can whip up a scrumptious batch of cranberry scones. Not to say that Nick can't, but why duplicate our efforts? He's the one who fills the propane tank and mixes marinade for grilled tri-tip. Our practical divide-and-conquer strategy plays to our strengths. Nick would rather push a mower around the lawn, check the tire pressure, or demonstrate the proper technique for hitting the seven ball into the side pocket. I'm okay being the guru of gift-wrap, farmers' markets and white sales.

Someone's gotta put that worm onto a fishhook and it's not going to be me.

To be successful at this parenting game, a wise couple merges their best qualities. If Mom is the heart of the home, then Dad is its backbone. Both roles are essential and operate best when working together. Mom may have the softer shoulder to cry on, but Dad's sturdier hugs are just as comforting.

Now—toenails freshly painted—I'm back at home. The house is quiet, but the fishing poles and vests tossed in the corner of the family room tell me my guys are back. I sneak through the house and find four anglers asleep on sofas and beds. A wrapped package in the refrigerator contains the results of their adventure. We will have fish to barbecue tonight.

During dinner they'll debate whose catch was the biggest, laugh about reeling in a ball of seaweed, and lament the yellowtail that wriggled free.

I'll laugh along, grateful that—unlike a certain fish—the special moments my sons caught with their dad didn't get away.

Color Coded

Pink is for girls. Blue is for boys. Or so we're told, but in an ever-evolving color-neutral society, even the toy world gets caught in the controversy. Recently the makers of the Easy-Bake Oven reassessed their color scheme. It didn't matter that, for five decades, famous chefs like Wolfgang Puck, Emeril Lagasse, and Bobby Flay overcame pink and purple play ovens to find success in their careers. Today, chef-hopefuls of either sex, eager to improve their novice cooking talents, have a palate of hues including blue, black, and silver—to choose from when buying the iconic oven.

As a young girl, I didn't own the once-light-bulb-heated range that now looks more like a microwave. I never bought one for any of my children, either. In fact, as a young mother, I never placed tea sets, glitter lipstick, or even training bras in my shopping cart. But if you need advice on where to get the best deals on trading cards, athletic supporters, or Wiffle ball bats, I'm your girl.

As mom to three sons, there's not much pink in my home. From the time the oldest was in diapers, my house was strewn with soccer balls, dump trucks, and building sets. There were no ribbon-dance wands, dream houses, or stuffed pandas tucked into corners of my family room. Naïvely, I lived through my thirties without ever trudging down the all-pink Barbie aisle in Toys "R" Us. Too much time spent in the Hot Wheels section, I guess.

I envied mothers who could French-braid their daughter's hair, attend jewelry design class, and spend time shopping for ballet slippers. While those women were splurging on pedicures, I was digging rocks, pogs (also known as milk caps) and unidentifiable gooey substances out of my sons' jeans pockets.

There's an upside to being the queen of the house, though. I was among the first subscribers to ESPN-the magazine, before most people even knew the sports publication existed. I can list eight ways a baseball player can get to first without getting a hit. (In case you're interested: walk, hit by pitch, error, catcher interference, fielder's choice, obstruction, dropped third strike—either wild pitch or passed ball). Not so long ago, I readily named all the characters in the *Thomas the Tank Engine* series. In a pinch, I could probably still come up with ten or so. I can hold my own in a game of Texas hold 'em.

Even in an evolving world where opportunities for both sexes continue to even out, mothers know their sons and daughters see things differently. Their interests, tastes, and preferences vary from the TV shows they like to their choices of what to wear to school—jeans and a T-shirt vs. lacy tops and leggings.

Whether you live on the pink or blue side of the fence—or if your family contains representation of both— it's tough mingling the two. The harder job may be teaching boys growing up in an all-guy household how to treat women and in an all-sister home, teaching girls how to relate to boys. My sons love their girl cousins and their friends' sisters, their first contacts with the other side.

Still, it's not the same as living with a female relative, other than Mom. (Mom's not really a girl, anyway.) No tiaras and doll babies were crammed in the toy closet alongside the trucks and car tracks. My sons didn't have tubes of mascara, lipstick, or a curling iron crowding the bathroom countertop.

They learned from their parents that pink or blue didn't equal weak or strong. It wasn't unusual for my fellas to witness me fixing sticky doors, replacing the car's broken sun visor, or digging out an overgrown honeysuckle bush.

Their dad throws in a load of laundry, cooks his Sunday morning breakfast scramble, and moves my yoga mat aside without so much as a whimper.

A balanced life uses every shade in your paint box. My sons know it doesn't matter who does the shopping, the cooking, or the cleaning as long as the work of the family is accomplished well and with love. Chicken casserole, frozen pizza, or chocolate chip cookies taste just as good in any color oven, no matter who's doing the baking.

Bumping Into the Message

My college-age son, Jake, home for spring break, took his truck in for routine maintenance, leaving him without wheels for the afternoon. So I offered him the use of my car for the day. I was surprised when he opted to walk to his destination instead of grabbing the keys and hopping into my 1997 Mercury Villager.

Sure, it's not a chick magnet, but it would get him safely from point A to point B. I'll admit to its tattered history as a part-time meal wagon. The smudges, spots, and grease stains imbedded in the fabric seats and carpet are remnants of Taco Tuesdays, sugar donuts, and bags of burgers and fries. It doesn't rack up the style points. There's no sunroof. The dashboard houses a cassette deck, not a CD player, the rear air conditioning doesn't work, and sometimes the auto door lock gets confused and unlocks itself. This minivan isn't sleek, shiny, or fast, but for the past fourteen years, it's been reliable, faithful, and functional—just like me.

Pondering his rejection, I stood in the doorway watching Jake walk down the street. Was he worried he'd be seen tooling around town in the same car where—a decade ago—he and his soccer pals left mustard fingerprints on the back seats? This car from his childhood shuttled him and his schoolmates to and from countless field trips, league games, and music lessons. It was the first place we'd look for missing cleats, dog leashes, footballs, and textbooks. He learned how to drive behind its steering wheel.

Puzzled, I strolled around the familiar minivan still parked in the driveway. True, it's missing a few things—a monthly payment, a never-empty gas tank, a recent wax job. Then a thought crossed my mind.

It wasn't the interior of my sun-faded spruce-green conveyance Jake snubbed. My guess was his issue was with its exterior.

Looking at my old wagon from a new perspective, I considered what it reveals about me as I rumble down the street. For starters, I have a pseudo-political bumper sticker that probably isn't in line with a twenty-something's thinking. Secondly, Jake and his two brothers are avid Chargers fans, just like their dad. My rear license plate holder touts my allegiance to a competing six-time Super Bowl-winning NFL team. And, to boot, mounted on the passenger's side is a rusty antenna where I've tied a foot-long strip of stars-and-stripes ribbon.

On my way to and from the Y the next day, I paid more attention to the variety of messages other drivers send via their bumpers. *My kid is an All Star Student at (school name here). I Support the Zoo, the Auto Club, KPBS. Baby (or Beagle) on Board. Sorry for Driving So Close in Front of You. Hang Up and Drive. I'd Rather Be: Hunting. (Fishing. Sleeping. Shopping.) Knowledge Speaks. Wisdom Listens.*

Now, every turn is a chance to uncover roadside insight, shared identity, new perspective, and maybe a laugh or two. Just this week, I sent a thumbs-up to a sedan from my native Pennsylvania, counted six license plate frames of fellow college alumnae and laughed at ironic pet humor (*Dogs have owners. Cats have staff*). I alternate between grins and grimaces on politically charged messages. Occasionally I'll even spy someone who shares my preference in football teams.

I'm not saying that now I welcome red lights as opportunities to learn. Or when I have a few extra minutes, I'm tempted to take a route dotted with stop signs so I can check out more bumpers. Scanning messages on the backsides of cars is a capricious, rudimentary, and inefficient way to get an education. Even so, these bits of wisdom and tidings have helped me declare—at least in my head—the car of my kids' childhood won't be the car of their mother's future.

After Jake and Seth graduate from college, I'm trading in old reliable for something sportier. Makes like Maserati, Porsche, Mercedes-Benz and BMW swim around in my thoughts. I see myself behind the wheel of a metallic storm-red convertible with leather interior, breathing in that new-car smell. I imagine my shoulder-length black hair waving in the breeze.

I will have earned that ragtop with seatbelts for two. I won't be offering the car of my dreams to my milkshake-sipping, soda-spilling, double-cheeseburger-eating offspring. Its immaculate image won't be sullied with stickers and decals, either.

Luckily there are messages my kids understand even if they're not plastered on a bumper: *Dad and I are spending your inheritance.*

Lines of Communication

It's Seth's turn to take out the trash.

Being sixteen, he often needs reminding. I thought about waiting until he notices that the can is overflowing and hope he'll take it out on his own. But I'm a realist. The price of gas will dip below $3 before that happens. I could write a note and tape it on the refrigerator door. He'll get hungry, eventually. Or I could walk upstairs to his room where he's on his computer and ask him face-to-face; but that's so 1970s.

I'm sure I'd get a quicker response if I used one of the electronic innovations he's familiar with. But I'm slow to change. Not that I'm against progress or anything. I cheered when the NBC peacock appeared in living color instead of black-and-white. I switched to music recorded on CDs instead of cassettes. I happily turned in my rotary dial phone for one with a keypad. Still, I'm leery when it comes to using cyberspace gizmos to communicate with my Generation Y children. If it weren't for my sons, I could pretty much avoid these instantaneous transmitters of information altogether.

When I was a teen, things were simple and direct. If the trash needed taking out, my mom shouted: *"Claire, take out the garbage."* I hollered back: *"I'll do it in a minute."* End of story. There were no high-tech messaging options. Back then, I was happy with a transistor radio, a dime in my pocket and a new Pee Chee folder (with that handy multiplication table printed on the inside). My friends and I thought Shake-a-Puddin' was cutting edge. On TV, we watched Captain Kirk and Mr. Spock use their starship communicator devices. Who knew that decades later, we'd be footing the bill for our own "communicator device" family plan.

My boys grew up underneath a technology tree. They are children of a computer-saturated generation where everything is a click away. A nanosecond is an eternity. Maturing right alongside laptops, cell phones, and the internet, they think it's quaint when I reminisce about telephone party lines. Nevertheless, my goal today is to get the trash taken out. If that means entering the world of electronic communications, I'll give it the old college try.

I consider (and dismiss): **Text messaging.** This takes me too long. I'd easily spend five minutes scrounging around for my reading glasses and then another five to plunk out "Takeouttrash." **Instant messenger.** My typing (or is it keyboarding?) speed is 70 wpm. This would be faster, but I'd have to sign on to IM and hope that Seth's logged on, too. **E-mail.** It might take a while before Seth checks his. **Cell phone.** I have to hope he answers when my name pops up on the caller ID.

As I see it, my limitless choices are thwarted by both technology and the end-user. But that's okay with me, because I prefer the handwritten word—one that isn't electronically conveyed. That's where our family whiteboard can't be beat. This non-technical communication device hangs on the wall near my kitchen, at the foot of the stairs. It's positioned at our home's crossroads, a perfect location for all the *news-you-can-use*.

This glossy melamine-coated board invites us to scrawl notes across its surface. Things like birthday greetings, opinions, predictions, reminders, football scores, and jokes are scribbled there. You can even find out what's for dinner.

I'm proud that this media center is not high-tech. No computer chips, LCD screens, or earbuds needed. The Geek Squad didn't install it. It doesn't need to be plugged in, downloaded, or recharged. But for my sons who were born in the era of instant everything, the whiteboard is a clever mix of old-school utility and newfangled slate.

Even though the board doesn't beep when a new message is posted, I know that this is the best place to leave a reminder for Seth. While I ponder whether to use the green or the blue dry-erase marker, my husband, Nick (also a product of the '70s) notices the overflowing trash can.

He hollers up the steps to Seth that it's trash day. *"And don't forget to feed the dogs, while you're at it,"* Nick adds. *"Sure, Dad,"* Seth yells back. *"I'll do it in a minute."*

I place the cap back on the marker and reach for my cell phone. From personal experience, I know how long that minute will be. I'll have plenty of time to send Seth that text message after all.

Mom, Put Your Oxygen Mask On First

The flight attendant stood at the front of the cabin, pointing to features on the aircraft as we readied for takeoff. She added a visual element to the humdrum voice coming from the speakers reminding passengers to fasten their seatbelts, turn off any electronics, and where to locate the nearest emergency exit.

This was my first solo flight as a mom. My eight-month-old son and I were on our way to visit Sadye, my sister. Shawn, still young enough not to require his own seat, was perched on my lap for the 80-minute journey from San Diego to Sacramento.

As part of the routine speech about FAA rules, our attendant held a coil of plastic tubing from an orange-coned mask in one hand as if it had dropped down from a compartment above, and demonstrated what to do in case the cabin lost pressure. "Grab the one hanging in front of you and put it on. Breathe normally," the overhead voice continued. "Parents put your oxygen mask on *before* you help your child with his."

My mind quickly weighed the plusses and minuses of putting Shawn's mask on him before I secured my own. *If an emergency really did happen, what would I do? How can I put my mask on first? What if I don't get to my son in time?* My maternal instinct, whirling with protective strategies, kicked in big-time.

Before my mental scenario took hold, though, the voice explained: "If you don't get oxygen, you can pass out or get disoriented and you won't be able to help your child."

In spite of my instinctive reaction to care for Shawn, that wasn't the safest choice. I needed to secure my own breathing first. This was a startling concept for this rookie mom to embrace—the importance of taking care of myself before I take care of my child.

I'd been absorbed by motherhood months before Shawn's birth. For me, it started when I first saw his heartbeat during a sonogram and felt his tiny feet kick inside my tummy. I prepared myself to love and nurture this little person long before my husband and I picked a name, a preschool, or a college fund. His welfare would always come before mine. For a flight attendant—or anyone else—to ask me to protect myself before taking care of my son was attempting miracles.

There's another occasion when mommies were called upon to do the impossible. This holiday rolls around on the second Sunday in May. You know it better as Mother's Day. The twenty-four hours when Mom's the top banana—pampered, fussed over, and honored as if she's an *American Idol* finalist.

From California to Connecticut, sleep-deprived women are lovingly served burned toast and lukewarm tea for breakfast. Homemade cards, bouquets of handpicked daisies, and warm hugs are the treasured gifts of the day. Dad has arranged for a bucket of chicken for dinner and the afternoon is spent doing what Mom likes to do—if only she could remember what that is.

It's hard for most moms to make the switch from caregiver to care-receiver. For 364 days a year, we're meal-planning, checkbook-balancing, nutrition-seeking beings, with just one mission—keeping our family safe, healthy, and happy. Our days are divided into many roles—wife,

mother, grandmother, sister, daughter, aunt, and friend—
and we do our best not to disappoint anyone. But on this
springtime Sunday, we're told to put away our day
planners, toilet brushes, and coupon caddies. We're coaxed
into relaxing while our kids take care of us.

Many Mother's Days have passed since that first
flight I took with Shawn. We arrived safely in Sacramento
without any oxygen masks popping out from overhead. But
that day, I left the plane with a new appreciation for why—
sometimes—it's okay for Mom to be first. A relaxed,
replenished mother is better equipped to take care of those
she cherishes.

Finding a few minutes to take a breath can seem
like an insurmountable task when you're raising children.
But if you plan it right, you can sneak "me-time moments"
into your day. My favorite breathers are a twenty-minute
yoga practice, meeting a friend for a mocha, or reading a
few pages of a captivating mystery. On a good day, I'm
soaking in a hot bubble bath, blissfully uninterrupted by the
demands of kids, husband, or to-do lists. Don't get me
wrong. Very few days play out like a 1960s TV sitcom.
Most of the time, I'm torn between hectic schedules and
conflicting demands. But if making time for me benefits
my family, then I'm willing to take one for the team.

This Mother's Day—and every day—if only for a
few minutes, *Put Your Oxygen Mask on First.* Those deep
breaths energize us to face burned toast, muddy tracks
across the kitchen floor, and that endless pile of
mismatched socks.

Caution: Mom At Work

I had stepped on Thomas and Percy—tank engines from my four-year-old son's toy train set—for the fifth time today.

Seth played with the miniature trains most of the afternoon, while nearby, I worked on my newspaper article about children at risk. We shared the cozy family-room workspace that now was littered with diesel engines named Mavis and Derek, railroad tracks, Harold the helicopter, and several other character trains from his favorite TV show.

My deadline was approaching in two days and I still needed to interview a child-welfare judge from the US District Court. While waiting for His Honor to return my early morning call, I'd spent my day researching facts, checking sources, folding the laundry, and refereeing disagreements.

It was 6:30 now—well past normal business hours. I needed to change from part-time investigative reporter to my more familiar role of cook-organizer-teacher-disciplinarian. Time to start dinner, pack lunches, and help my 13-year-old with his science project. Nick would be home soon to take some of the pressure off.

I knelt on the carpet next to Seth and tossed metal trains into a plastic container, when the phone rang. With each clatter of metal hitting plastic, Seth heard my feelings expressed verbally about the mess strewn across the floor.

That's when I looked up and saw eight-year-old Jake holding the portable phone. The person on the other end had heard every word of my loud discourse about the values of cleaning up after yourself.

"Who is it?" I snapped.

"I don't know, Mom. Some man asking for you," he said, handing me the phone as he scooted out of the room for a quick getaway.

"Hello?"

"Claire Fadden?"

"Yes, this is Claire."

"This is Judge Jones. I'm returning your call. My secretary said you wanted to talk to me about our report on children as victims of violence."

My stomach sank. Instead of showing myself as a professional writer prepared for an interview, I suddenly felt like someone who could be ordered to appear before him. I hoped to hear from the judge before the craziness of the dinner hour hit, but I suppose that his day was as jam-packed as mine. Struggling to ask pertinent questions, I wondered if he thought I sounded like some of the parents he had seen in his court.

Rewind the clock to nine years earlier when I was working full-time as promotions manager for a world-renowned San Diego tourist attraction. During a crazy, hectic morning of getting ready, Shawn, who was four at the time, asked me if I liked the Mother's Day necklace he'd made for me at preschool.

"Of course, I do, Shawn." I vigorously assured him with a hug. "I love it. It's my favorite necklace."

"Then why don't you ever wear it?" he asked, pointing to where it hung from my dresser mirror.

Rather than explain to him why it didn't go with my business suit, I took off my strand of freshwater pearls. As he beamed his approval, I enthusiastically replaced them with Shawn's handmade bauble.

I'll change back to the pearls after I drop Shawn off at preschool, I thought.

On the drive to the office, my thoughts switched to marketing guru, but in my rush to get to work on time, I forgot to make the same change in the appearance department. My jewelry was still in Mom-mode when I walked into the weekly advertising staff meeting. Shawn's circle of turquoise-colored yarn, dotted with a dozen or so pink, orange, and green Fruit Loops—dangled from my neck as the executive director leaned across the conference room table and asked: "Are you wearing cereal?" Proudly, I told him that I was.

During my years of pursuing dual roles as mother/career woman, I've done my best to merge the two. Since the time Shawn was old enough to say "Mommy," I've explored nearly every type of working arrangement: 1) full-time, stay-at-home mom; 2) full-time, at-the-office mom; 3) part-time worker/full-time mom and 4) full-time, work-at-home mother.

I've come full circle to find my career/life balance as a mother working from home. It's a tightrope walk to mix the joys of motherhood with the rewards of freelance writing. Neither job offers regular hours, sick leave, vacation, or a 401K. Both promise fulfillment in other, less concrete ways. As a journalist, I write about interesting people, places, and things; smile when I see my byline in print; and hope that my articles touch the reader.

It's the incalculable benefits of being a mother that I treasure most, though. Sticky kisses, late-night "I love yous" and finger-painted birthday cards are a few of the perks I've received from my primary occupation.

So what if my retirement portfolio will limit me to vacationing in Tucson instead of Tuscany. I have the best job in the world. What other career comes with an endless supply of unanswerable questions, midnight trips to the pharmacy, a client who has used your skirt hem as a tissue, and a necklace you could eat if you ran short on lunch money?

Look, Mom, Nine Cavities!

What started out as a routine dental checkup with my then-four-year-old son Seth ended up as a parenting wake-up call. In a matter of mere minutes, my preschooler with a heart-melting smile had transformed into a kid with nine cavities. Nine—that's one for every player position on a baseball field. I felt my supermom smile turn into a frown as our dentist broke the bad news to me.

"This little boy isn't taking care of his teeth," Dr. H said. His glare translated to *Mom, you're not doing your job*.

This is the same Dr. H. I've entrusted my own pearly whites to since I was seventeen. The same dentist who pulled out my wisdom teeth, welcomed my husband Nick as a new patient, followed by each of my boys as they reached the age when their teeth required the care of a professional.

I had no defense. No reasonable way to excuse the little black pits that had taken hold in my youngest's mouth. Somehow, between the time Seth's two bottom teeth popped out and that day, I'd lost control of his dental well-being. Our routine of me brushing his teeth morning and night using his *Thomas the Tank Engine* toothbrush had been replaced, it seems, with no brushing at all.

Seth could hardly wait to get home and brag to our previous record holder—eight-year-old brother Jake—that he had topped him for most cavities in one visit. Seth claimed the dreadful title by shattering Jake's three-cavity visit with his nine. Dr. H. tried to minimize the blow by saying that a couple of the cavities were little ones, but his message was clear—dental hygiene had reached a new low at the Fadden home.

This slick preschool-sized salesman convinced me that he was big enough to take care of his teeth. He wanted to be just like his older brothers, Shawn and Jake. But under Seth's dental care management, his healthy teeth had become a home to the tooth decay monster. Was my son in this situation because I'd fallen for the wet-toothbrush trick too many times, or because Seth was the youngest and I'd gotten lax in my parenting? My days were full with three kids and a job. Or was it because I had naïvely put my faith in the words of wisdom from a four-year-old declaring: "Mom, I can do this myself."

Gullible, yes. Hearing what I wanted to hear, probably. But the truth bit down on me like an alligator clenching its prey. This little step on the path of letting him grow up and be responsible had backfired. Even though he wanted to be treated like his big brothers, he was too young to be the sole caretaker of his teeth. Seth and I had learned this painful lesson nine times over.

Before he was to be destined to a lifetime of gumming his food, I knew I had to reclaim this territory. But I couldn't do it by taking away a responsibility that had already been conferred. And I couldn't make Seth the only focus of my plan. I wanted to get his attention as well as the other two before this quest-for-cavity-king got out of control. I certainly didn't want Shawn or Jake trying to top Seth's record-setting efforts.

That's when I decided to spin this cavity contest in a positive direction. I had to put my money where their mouths were and offer a reward—$50 cash money—to any son with a cavity-free checkup. In the spirit of encouraging a good effort, $25 would come their way if one cavity managed to sneak in, but if you had two or more cavities, you got zilch and Mom on your case.

At our next scheduled appointment, I told Dr. H and his hygienist about my new plan. They thought it was a great idea and pulled for Shawn, Jake, and Seth to succeed. It wasn't long before I began to pay out on this bet. More often than not, I'd hear: "Look Mom, no cavities." And it was hard to say who enjoyed telling me the news—my kids or the dental team.

The brothers still compete. Random contests for the loudest burp, the smelliest socks, and the stupidest nickname are still part of our lives.

Fortunately, there's no one seeking the title of cavity king anymore. It didn't take long for these smart cookies to figure out that cash in your pocket is much more appealing than a mouth full of fillings. Now that's something I can smile about.

MOM = Made of Money

It happened in a flash at a mall not far from my home. The realization that I had become one of those mothers—a woman who indulges her young with too much, wanting to make sure they have everything. Unwittingly, I was becoming the kind of mother whose kids aren't prepared for adulthood.

The truth hit me like two weeks' worth of dirty clothes, tumbling down my laundry chute. Somewhere along the line, while I was performing day-to-day mothering duties, my three sons grew up thinking that MOM stood for "Made of Money." I'm not sure when this happened, but I knew how. It wasn't such a stretch for my kids to equate MOM with money. Nowadays, everything is labeled with an acronym. Kids watch DVDs, teams play OT and we use the ATM. It was a natural progression for MOM to mean Made of Money.

This wasn't the definition of motherhood I learned from my mom Florence. Quite the opposite. She raised me to be independent and self-sufficient. If there was something special I wanted, I paid for it with my babysitting money. I never considered using her purse as the means to buy stuff.

I shoulder the blame for teaching my sons this flawed meaning. Being a loving (overindulgent) mom, it was rare that I'd say no to a Slurpee, a new game, or an ice cream cone at Cold Stone Creamery. What better way to show my love than through confections, surprises, and goodies? How could I insist that my sons learn the value of a dollar by spending their own?

It wasn't that they couldn't afford to pay for their extras. They had allowance, birthday-money and cash they'd earned doing other chores. It was taking up space in their wallets, pockets, and piggybanks. The truth was, it made me feel good to be seen as the benefactor. There were many chances for my guys to learn firsthand about money management, but I was a reluctant teacher.

It wasn't until I was sneaker-shopping with thirteen-year-old Seth that I realized what I had unknowingly created. There it was displayed before me in rubber, canvas, and shoelaces, the fitting result of saying *yes* more often than saying *no*. I had become an OP; an overindulgent parent. The truth snuck up on me as slowly and quietly as post-holiday pounds, and hit just as hard.

As I sat on the store bench eyeing a wall of sneakers with descriptions like turbo, max, zoom, and vapor, I sensed that this outing would lead to an expensive entry in my checkbook. Seth was nearby, cradling a pair the way I would expect him to hold a kitten or a fallen bird— tenderly, lovingly, carefully. In his hands were shoes with a price tag that rivals our monthly gas and electric bill. I realized that sneakers were more than footgear to teenagers. I knew that they don't wear them just to protect their feet. Sporting the right athletic shoe was a fashion statement, but I was reluctant to be the financing behind that big of a statement.

As I stared at the three-figure cost, I commented in my official Mom voice: *Do you think I'm made of money?* Without a word, the puzzled glaze that washed over my son's face gave me his answer: *Of course. Why wouldn't I?* And I had to agree. All his life I had been his prime source of comfort, affection, and funding. The only mother he knew was a habitual OP. He'd seen it firsthand and—being

the youngest of three—witnessed it when he watched how his older brothers were treated. Short of buying a condo in the Bahamas, he knew that Mom and Dad would provide unconditional support, love, and money. He was about to find out that two out of three ain't bad. Support and love were guaranteed, but his level of funding was about to take a big hit.

After a rather long and overdue discussion about the value of a dollar—I think I even threw in my mom's line: *You know it doesn't grow on trees*—we came to an understanding. There was a maximum price I would pay. Seth could still pick whatever shoes he wanted, but anything over that amount would come out of his pocket. A few facial contortions later, he made a different shoe selection, one that fit within the budget.

It's been months since my catharsis at the mall. I'm happy to report that, with perseverance, self-reflection, and determination, I'm on the road to recovery. Admitting that I had become an OP was the first step.

My sons now know that MOM doesn't always stand for "Made of Money." As they observe my changing behavior, I hope they'll also realize that their sometimes penny-pinching MOM is doing her best to *mold outstanding men.*

Have Kids. Gotta Travel.

From the driver's seat of my green Mercury
Villager, I smile at the woman in the navy-blue Honda
Civic. I'm not sure if it's Teresa, Connie, or Melanie, but I
know that the car is familiar. So I wave after dropping my
son Seth off at school. It's quite possible that I don't know
the driver of the car, but she waves back anyway.

It's early in the day. I'm still shaking off sleep when
I realize that I haven't even brushed my teeth yet. It's a
good thing that my morning socializing takes place from
behind a steering wheel.

That's how it is when you're the mother of the
Young and Unlicensed who depend on you for their
transportation. For the better part of the daylight hours, we
carpooling moms operate from a bucket seat and view the
world through a smudged windshield. Our glamorous life
of pickup and delivery rivals the schedule of most UPS
drivers. It benefits us to remember what make and model
our friends drive because it's easier to recognize them that
way. A silver Grand Cherokee (Suzie) or a white Sonata
(Alma) gets a smile and a friendly hand gesture from me
most mornings.

We've become our car. Right now my friends see
me as a minivan, but I know that the woman inside is really
a sports car. Maybe someday I'll shed this guise of
traditional stability and opt for the rogue scampiness of a
Porsche. I daydream about driving past other SUV-moms

waiting in the Y's parking lot and waving to them from inside a red Maserati Spyder.

Before marriage and kids, I drove a sleek two-door silver Toyota Celica. It had a stick shift and just enough room for me, my load of college books and a passenger, should I decide to have one. Now, my vehicle has seatbelts for seven, space for soccer balls and goals, a bicycle, nine bags of groceries, and a couple dogs. My minivan is an automatic. That makes it much easier and a lot less fun to drive on hills and to parallel park.

Like other moms, my earliest days of motherhood were brimming with kid-related transportation challenges. That's when my trio of sons were in their car seat years (under six and sixty pounds). Even the easiest task, like picking up a gallon of milk, involved work, patience, and pre-planning. By the time everyone was buckled in, I would be questioning the need for milk, diapers, or food of any kind. I learned quickly that if the errand I was running didn't offer a drive-thru, we didn't need to go. I just waited until Nick came home from work, and off I'd go—alone.

I unearthed lots of drive-thru options, other than fast food. I could bank, pick up prescriptions, drop off dry cleaning and even treat myself to a double chocolate latte on those days when I needed a boost. Without having to get out of the car, I could mail letters at the post office, drop off overdue books at the library and return movies at the local video rental shop.

Of course there were errands that had to be done before Nick was home, at places where there were no drive-thrus. On those rare occasions, I would focus my energies on accomplishing the goal, factoring in enough time to load, unload, load, and reload my kiddies in the car. Frequently the loading took much longer than the task at hand.

As the boys got older, the errand-running and play dates turned into carpooling to football practice, music lessons, catechism class, and club meetings. Taking the guys to (and from) their activities left me little time in between to return home, start dinner, and throw in a load of whites. It made more sense to just hang out.

So I—being the resourceful multi-tasker that every mom evolves into by the time her youngest is in kindergarten—provided myself with an emergency road kit. Just a few things to keep me busy while I waited for guitar lessons to end. No jumper cables, flares, or radiator coolant in this tote bag. Instead, to help pass the time, I packed stationery to write overdue thank-you notes, a half-read Janet Evanovich novel, snacks for the famished, crayons and coloring books to keep others entertained, and that week's sale ads.

Today, two of my three sons are licensed drivers. The third is not far off from becoming a member of the driving public. My days of car seats, carpools, and drop-offs are coming to a close. I find myself thinking about spending afternoons sitting at the neighborhood street-side café, leisurely sipping a smoothie and thumbing through this month's issue of *Real Simple*. From my vantage point, I'll be able to see my friends' cars as they drive by on their way to an orthodontist appointment or some other child-related event.

Of course I'll wave and I'll understand if they don't wave back. Since I'm not in my car, it might be hard for them to recognize me.

Memo From a Team Mom

It's the start of another season. Baseball, soccer, football, basketball, it doesn't matter. I'm the mother of three sons, so some sport is always being played. I dust off my boys' cleats, find their gloves, and locate the air pump. A new season, a fresh start. And with the beginning of every sport comes new opportunity—even for parents.

A chance to volunteer to be the team mom.

This isn't a job to be taken lightly. The team mom has many important duties and she does pose, along with the coaches, in the team picture. She's an important part of the team.

I've been team mom more than a few times. In fact, I've held the title so often, that my son Jake felt the need to write about it in a homemade M-O-T-H-E-R's Day card. The T stands for Team Mom. According to Jake: *"My mom is ALWAYS the Team mom."* In his eyes, this is one of my best qualities.

As my sons grow, opportunities to be team mom come less frequently. Before long, I'll be out of my team-mothering prime. That's why I feel it's my duty to prepare the next generation of team moms. With countless years of Team Motherhood under my belt (and nacho cheese sauce under my nails), some moms say that makes me experienced. I say it's time for someone else to get experienced.

Every mom deserves a chance to earn her T, too. So, with that goal in mind, I've condensed what I've learned during my years of team motherhood into these five points:

1) Plan ahead. Not only do you have to be organized, but you have to organize some twelve to fifteen players, ranging in ages from four to fourteen, and their parents.

2) Don't print copies of the team roster too soon. In your zeal to produce your team's roster—noting all the parents' first names and each player's jersey number—you may overlook a few things. Trust me, finishing the roster usually takes two or three tries before you get it right. Invariably, someone's name is misspelled or another player is added.

3) The Snack Schedule! Make no mistake; this IS the most important and most stressful team mom task. If you don't think so, hang around after any T-ball game when the snack mom (or dad) didn't show. You'll never see so many sad faces as parents rush to 7-Eleven to purchase last-minute treats. Don't mess with the snack schedule. Print many copies and always have one handy, so you can remind parents of their snack day!

4) Be prepared to: orchestrate picture day, solidify a snack-bar duty schedule, collect money from the candy drive, solicit sponsorships, plan the end-of-the-season party and purchase a gift for the coach.

5) What they *won't* tell you about being a team mom: Come prepared with a needle and thread, Band-Aids, ice packs, sunflower seeds, a Sharpie, and a sympathetic ear. During my team-mothering tenure, I've needed all of those items. I've sewn the catcher's gear back together in between innings (he was still wearing it). As an injured player sat on the bench, I got a game ball signed by the entire team without him knowing. I made certain the coach

played Dougie because his uncle visiting from Idaho was in the stands.

Being team mom takes a lot of time, a lot of effort and a lot of love. A love I willingly share with my children and their teammates. I want to savor this time—make it last like the final two minutes of an NFL game.

Being team mom gets me in the action while my boys still think I'm cool. That's why earning my T is so special. My sons will only issue these *patches from the heart* for a limited time. And only during baseball (basketball, football, soccer) season.

For the Love of Leftovers

"All we ever eat is leftovers!"
--the Fadden brothers, in search of food

My sons insist that leftovers are the only food served in our house. Over the years, this rally cry for action from Shawn, Jake and Seth usually amounts to a request for fast food. This day, I unwisely challenge their assertion.

"You have to have a home-cooked meal in order for the leftovers to exist," I insist. "That's why they call them leftovers. They're *left over!*"

Jake stands, leaning against the inside of the refrigerator door, waiting for something savory to appear before him. Maybe he thinks that if he waits long enough, a double cheese and pepperoni pizza from Domino's will appear. Heavy sigh. Alas, all he can find is the leftover chicken fajitas and a mystery casserole he didn't want to eat the first time I served it.

About this time the real controversy sets in while they continue to question ever eating the original meals.

"Do you think I get them from other moms who cooked and saved their leftovers for us?" No response. "You think Mrs. Wagner spent her Sunday making pot roast, so you'd have leftovers for lunch on Monday?" Still no response. "Not every meal can be a visit to In–N–Out Burger," I lament, knowing this will get a retort.

"Why not?" questions twelve-year-old Seth, peering around his brother's shoulder in the hopes that with both of them concentrating, the pizza will surface. "That's what a hamburger is all about."

This comment slices through my "how-to-be-a-conscientious-mom" gene. "A good mother doesn't take her kids to fast food restaurants seven times a week," I reply, not sure that I've mounted a winning argument. "What kind of a mom would I be?"

"You'd be the best mom!" they both chime.

Unconvinced, I reach for my copy of the *100 Greatest Leftover Recipes*.

Jake selects a Tupperware bowl, lifts the lid, sniffs, and puts it back on the shelf. Conceding defeat, Seth has already walked to the pantry, pulled out a box of Lucky Charms and is headed back to the fridge for the milk.

Jake relents, too. The makings of a turkey and cheese sandwich start to hit the countertop.

I continue on, boasting the inherent worth of leftovers. "A creative mom can make five different meals out of one whole chicken," I say, hoping to impress them with this fact. The impression was somewhat like touting the merits of putting all your dirty clothes down the laundry chute if you wanted them washed—good in theory, lousy in practice.

Collective grunts echo through cereal crunches and sandwich smacks. Unfazed, I leaf through the cookbook's pages hoping for a revelation.

"Yeah, that's right," I enthuse. "Like the fajitas in the fridge. I can also make fried chicken, barbecued chicken pizza, chicken and rice soup, and chicken salad, for less than the cost of four double-doubles, fries, and shakes." I rest my case.

"From one measly chicken," Seth nods in disbelief. "I don't want to eat five different kinds of chicken anyway, Mom. And you've never made chicken and rice soup," he charges.

"Unless you're canning it with a Campbell's label," Jake suggests.

Shawn bounds into the kitchen, home from college for the weekend. This twenty-year-old joyfully explores our land of leftovers. Meatloaf from last Thursday; cheeseburger soup from Wednesday; a taco casserole, not sure of the date—it's all good.

"What's wrong with you guys?" he says, loading up his plate of fajitas, with some rice that I had forgotten was in there.

He has an earned respect for leftovers. With a quest for higher learning and living on his own, Shawn developed an appreciation for food—free food, leftover or not— when he was the one responsible for cooking it.

"Let me check that first, Shawn," I say, making sure the green-tinted seasoning was the one that came in the Rice-a-Roni package.

"You guys don't know how good you have it. All this food for free, and you're complaining. Mom shops for it, pays for it, and cooks it. All you two have to do is eat it." He shoves a big bite of a fajita-covered tortilla in his mouth.

His siblings are not convinced. Apart from Thanksgiving turkey and mashed potatoes, there's little worth eating that's been made the day before, pizza notwithstanding. Nothing Shawn says convinces his younger brothers.

It was just a few short months ago that Shawn, too, thought leftovers were as appetizing as dental floss. Now, whenever he's home from college, he excitedly scours the refrigerator in the hopes of a delicious find, one that isn't packaged in foam. He appreciates the little things living at home signify: gas in the car, clean towels, and all the free food you can eat. But like every life lesson, Shawn's love of leftovers came through trial and error. He learned the only way any of us can, through living it.

His brothers will learn too, in their own time, in the hallowed halls of dormitories and frat houses, and on weekend visits back home.

"Mother U R the GR8ST"

I will probably never be named Mother of the Year and that's okay with me.

I'm happiest when I am praised, even for a moment, by one of my three sons. Kudos from my trio of boys don't emerge from solving society's problems. I haven't unearthed a software solution to block spam, a plan to lower the price of gas, or even an easy way to remove Orange Blast Gatorade stains from the front of baseball uniforms. You won't see my name listed alongside great women like Clara Barton, Mother Teresa, or Marie Curie. But I am remembered by my boys for less notable, but infinitely more important reasons.

For example, over the years, I've heard: "Mom, you're awesome." (*Shawn, when I found his missing soccer cleats.*) "Claire, you're clutch" (*Jake, after having his sweatshirt mended.*) or "Mom, you rock!" (*any of them upon discovering a full bag of peanut butter M&Ms in the pantry*). The highlight, though, was the day my twelve-year-old, Seth, declared me the greatest.

The title of this essay comes from a reply to an e-mail I sent him. Now, you might ask why I'm e-mailing my son whose bedroom is less than 100 feet away from my own. But these are techno days and sometimes e-mail is the easiest way to supply him with information or get his attention.

Excitedly I clicked open this e-mail to learn what wonderful, motherly thing I had done to warrant such a declaration. Was it the fact that Seth's PE clothes were clean and ready to go every Monday morning? Maybe it was the way I had shredded my Sunday paper into confetti searching for pictures of food items to match his Spanish word list. It could have been an acknowledgement of the miles and miles I've put on my old Villager minivan, not to mention my own chassis, hauling him from basketball, soccer, or football practice. But alas, no. None of these routine, yet important Mom tasks garnered me Seth's proclamation.

It was just a little thing I had done during the course of my daily duties; finding locations of Dairy Queens in San Diego County and e-mailing them to him. An afterthought to me, but huge news to my youngest.

After returning from his summer vacation in Sacramento, Seth told me that he loved to go to DQ, a place his Aunt Sadye took him for ice cream Blizzards, burgers, and hot dogs. Wanting to maintain my spot as number one—and not wanting to be outdone by my sister—I invited Seth to lunch one winter afternoon. We ended up at what I thought was the nearest DQ, only to find that the ice cream and burger joint was now a haven for fried-chicken lovers. We settled for chicken fingers and fries. Disappointment painted Seth's face but he didn't complain. With his eyes cast down, he slowly dipped his chicken into ranch dressing and nibbled his fries.

I said nothing, but I knew that my son's happiness was just a Google search away. A few moments at my PC would mean hours of future fast-food happiness for the Fadden family.

Even though the message was only five words long (two of which were the letters), Seth's brief e-mail taught me a lot about being a mom. In a flash, it emanated what's important to Seth. I know he appreciates the everyday things I do for him—dinner on the table, allowance on Fridays, and clean underwear.

But his e-mail signaled another message. What's top priority to me (getting your homework done) is probably not what's number one with him (shooting some hoops). Fortunately there's room for both kinds of *important*—good study habits and jaunts out for caramel frappuccinos; washing behind your ears and staying up too late; taking out the over-flowing trash; and sock wars. With just a few keystrokes (twenty, to be exact) Seth showed me that somewhere amid the busyness of daily living, mother and son still connect—whether it's via the internet, or over milkshakes.

In between laundry and grocery shopping, packing lunches, and signing permission slips, I'm looking beyond the day-to-day tasks for those award-winning mom moments. These chances don't come along every day, but they're there if I look for them—rare opportunities to be nominated for a Mom-of-the-Year (or at least of the Day) award.

So when the magic hits again and I garner another glowing e-mail from Seth, or a compliment from Shawn or a thank-you from Jake, I'll just take it in stride.

But on the inside I'll be the woman SFE2E (smiling from ear-to-ear) because I'm OLM (one lucky mom).

Motherhood's Lesson Plan

Nick and I had been married about a year and a half. We were still getting used to the idea of being Mr. and Mrs., sharing decisions like picking out a couch and learning to stay on a budget.

He worked as a restaurant manager while I finished up my BS in Journalism at San Diego State. Courses like "Libel Law and the Media" and "Writing for Publication" filled my mind and my time. That's when it first hit: a thick sensation in the bottom of my stomach. At first, I thought it was the flu. The symptoms started slowly, just nipped at me the first couple mornings, but by the end of the week, I was in bed, cradling a bucket under my head. Not even dry toast was my friend.

Morning sickness, afternoon sickness, evening sickness and every-other-time-of-the-day-sickness. Little did I realize that this signaled my headlong plunge into the earliest stages of motherhood's lesson plan. This was nature's way of getting my attention. A major change was underway.

In those early weeks before my first son was born and I nibbled crackers to keep my stomach in place, I didn't realize that I was in the infant stages of parenting. This intense on-the-job training course graduated me from infant to toddler to preschool to teen mothering. Each of my studies stayed right in step with what Shawn was learning. The days when I made anxious visits to the bathroom to check on a potty trainee taught me to think on a preschool level. Each late-night chorus of the *Itsy Bitsy Spider* falling on the ears of a listener who didn't want to go to bed yet, was teaching patience. And every time I said: "Take one piece of candy now and we'll save the rest for later," promoted me to the next age and stage of motherhood.

Disguised as normal life, these moments were my learn-as-you-go studies. A unique mixture of trial-and-error, wisdom from other moms, visits to the pediatrician and frequent thumbings through *Parenting for Dummies* guides. Advanced courses like removing a bee's stinger from a squirming first grader's head, cutting chewing gum out of a four-year-old's hair and even learning why a fourteen-year-old needs X-box Live were necessary. Each one contributed to the strong foundation of strength, courage, perseverance, humor, and knowledge (not to mention prayer) I'd need in the years to come.

Just a week ago, I unexpectedly shared this insight with my niece Sara, a young mother of two. As our family's home-decorating diva, Sara frequently shares her expertise with me about everything from how to select wall paint to keeping my African violets healthy. My most recent query was about picture frames. Her response started out: "I can't believe I'm sitting here at one in the morning answering my e-mails, but Roman is teething and when he can't sleep, I don't get to, either."

I replied to her note by letting her in on a little secret: Roman, in his infinite wisdom (at the age of twenty-two months) wasn't just breaking in molars. He was also breaking her in for his double-digit years. Those years that take more stamina and skill than changing any poopy diaper ever would. These late nights with Roman were just prep for the bigger stuff; his first week away at camp, his first date, the day he takes his driving test (in a mere fourteen years or so) and tons of other fun calamities he hasn't even planned yet.

It's no coincidence that by the time Roman presents Sara with these new challenges, she'll have more than thirteen years parenting experience to draw upon. That's more on-the-job training that any doctor gets before she opens her practice. It's all part of the lesson plan.

Sara is immersed in on-the-spot parenting. She's learning her mommy skills at the same rate her children (Sadye, 5 and Roman) are growing. Sara e-mailed me back several days later, once again during the middle of the night. She didn't see the activities that she was currently involved in—Roman's teething worries and finding Sadye's favorite mermaid outfit—as a path to acquiring the skills for mothering a fifteen- and a twelve-year-old. "That's just too far off in the future to think about," she said. But in her next sentence, she agreed to being more prepared now as a mom than she was five years ago.

A preview of Sara's Year-Six Curriculum: finding objects that begin with the letter M, Q, and X (kindergarten homework), recognizing the difference between James and Edward (trains from the *Thomas the Tank Engine* series) and whatever else Sadye and Roman concoct.

I assured Sara that by the time she's making trips to the orthodontist, helping with freshman English, and planning for prom night, she'll be one well-educated mom.

A Mother's Malady

I'm sick. Unless you're a teenager I've given birth to, though, you might not notice. There's no cough, I don't have a rash, and I'm not the one in pain. There's no remedy to treat the symptoms and my doctor can't give me a prescription. Only time will cure my malady.

Since I've been a mom, I've been afflicted with this condition twice before—once when Shawn was about thirteen and then some four years later, coincidentally when Jake was thirteen. The onset of this disorder, which I've termed *High School Parentitis (HSP)*, only strikes adults while their children are teens. It's more commonly seen in women, but men are also affected.

Fortunately, this temporary parental disorder seems to diminish greatly once your child reaches adulthood. It disappears altogether when they become parents.

As the mom of three sons, two who are mostly through their teen years, I should have suspected that I would succumb once again. The onslaught of the illness hit right about the time my youngest, Seth, approached fourteen and was just months away from being a freshman in high school.

I remember when this cherub-cheeked face called me *princess*, begged me to play *Thomas the Tank Engine* and even asked why my hair went in loops. I have naturally curly hair. Barely a decade later, that same face, now sporting braces and indications of facial hair, calls me old-fashioned and thinks my only purpose in life is to embarrass him in front of his friends.

I knew I was in the early stages of *HSP* a couple months ago when I asked to chaperone an eighth-grade field trip. The look on Seth's face sent me scurrying to a mirror to see if I had grown a third eye or if my hair had set itself on fire. Only after much negotiation—and a guaranteed visit to Jamba Juice—did I secure my spot on this trip to Old Town. Seth relented after I promised that: 1) I wouldn't wear my "I'm Seth's Mom" T-shirt; 2) I wouldn't kiss him in front of his friends—especially the girls; and 3) I would never ask to chaperone any of his activities, ever again.

I can't blame him for not wanting his friends to see his mom in this condition. In fact, I almost understand his side—despite what he thinks, I wasn't born old. But the truth is since I'm a mom, I act like a mom. I've been this way since the doctor handed over my firstborn and said, "Here you go!" That's when the maternal stuff kicked in. By the time Shawn was in kindergarten, I was mothering at full tilt.

Like all moms, I'm hard-wired to care, to educate, to nurture, to nourish, and to love. Traits that aren't treasured by teens—in fact, they're as welcome as a pimple on prom night. So on the morning of the field trip, Seth's worst fears were realized when I displayed these *HSP* behaviors.

Not only did I show up with a jacket for Seth, but I toted an extra one along for one of his friends.

Since everyone had to sit two to a seat on the bus, Seth was stuck sitting next to me.

And when I requested my group of boys to learn something on the field trip, my disease moved to the advanced stages. While others spent time in the shops, my bunch was lodged in the tiny Mason Street School, circa 1865, comparing school supplies: chalk and wooden-framed slate vs. keyboard and computer screen. "Really fun, Mom."

Moms smooth things over with food, so after our history lesson, I treated the guys to nachos, tacos, and enchiladas. Even though the boys had packed sack lunches, we gathered around an umbrella-topped table to munch Mexican food. For a moment, I felt like I might be part of the gang. The kids were polite and talkative. But as I dipped my chip into the guacamole, I knew that my days of fitting in with thirteen-year-old boys had passed.

This once-groovy and hip girl of the '70s is no longer *all that* in the eyes of the under-sixteen set.

But it's all good. I'm not supposed to be one of the dudes. My role—my priority—is to be Seth's mom, old-fashioned or not. And I'm down with that. Seth has lots of friends, but only one set of parents. So, if his dad and I must suffer through another bout of *HSP*, so be it. We can handle it. We've recovered twice before.

That's the good news.

The not-so-good news is that there is an illness that often follows *HSP*. It takes on a different form and the symptoms aren't so personal. Your kids want to be seen with you. In fact, they may be more interested in you—and your wallet—than you wish.

I've named this financially-focused disability *painintheparentscheckbook (PPCB)*. It appears immediately after high school graduation and lasts about four years, if you're lucky.

Bloopers, Blunders, and Other Memorable Moments from the

Motherhood Hall of Shame

No woman truly appreciates her mom until she's a mother herself. I didn't realize how wise and patient my mother was until I was a grown woman, facing my own set of pint-sized critics. From my trio of boys, I've been the target of so many judgmental eye-rolls that you'd think their eyes would be sore.

I shouldn't complain. I, too, rolled my brown eyes and snickered under my breath at my mother on occasion. Okay, a lot of occasions. Of course, at sixteen, I knew more than this woman who had already survived raising my older brothers and sister, owned her own home, and was loaning me money to buy my first car. But Mom was a bit square. She would refer to low-riding as low-driving, she thought that "shake your booty" was something babies did with their feet, and she never let me get away with the argument: *Liz's mom is letting her go to the party.*

Even though I attempt to dodge the inevitable blunders of mom-hood, I realize that my guys have more ammunition than I care to admit. I've pulled a few well-intentioned bloopers in my time, all in the name of being a good mom. Here are a few past performances that could land me in the Motherhood Hall of Shame.

-- Blue Jell-O Aquariums (complete with floating gummy fish). In my quest to outdo other preschool moms, and celebrate Jake's birthday, I lovingly made twenty-four individual clear plastic cups of blue Jell-O. After the snack-time celebration, the tiny tots were released to the playground. I collected approximately twenty mostly-uneaten gelatin aquariums left on the preschool lunch table. Many still had plastic spoons harpooned in them, looking like they were the victims of an undersea exploration gone awry. Miss Diane then told me that no one likes blue gelatin and only a few kids really liked gummy anything. "Ice cream sandwiches would have been better," a four-year-old Jake told me later.

— A Mistake on Wheels. Concerned that my middle-schooler Seth was suffering from hauling a heavy load of textbooks on his back, I surprised him with a teal-colored rolling backpack. I didn't know that *rolling backpack* was synonymous with *nerd*. My vision was to relieve his backbreaking load. Seemed like a reasonable solution. On Monday, he reluctantly rolled the backpack from the car and out of my line of vision. By day two, the wheeled pack was compacted into a regular-size backpack and hoisted onto Seth's back. He toted his textbooks inside this heavier version. By Friday, after schooling me *about backpack truths and fitting in*, a smiling yet book-laden Seth was back to hauling around his navy blue JanSport.

--Injured Player/Worried Mom. I learned the hard way that walking to the players' bench during the middle of a high-school varsity football game to check on your son is a big no-no. It doesn't matter if your child was just knocked out on the previous play. My reward for concern and worry: the most definite "I'm-okay. Go-back-to-the-stands" stink eye ever known to mom-kind.

--Attempting an "Adventure in Dining." Cooking isn't my strong suit, but I try to feed my family healthy meals. So my special Tuna Surprise won't ever be featured in *Bon Appétit!* I'm okay with that. Shawn claims that the real surprise was that anyone ate it.

My most recent nomination to the Hall involved buying all three boys corduroy jackets for Christmas. In a tone that left me never wanting to purchase outerwear again, I was informed that corduroy isn't worn by anyone under forty, no matter how warm and cozy.

It's a hard fact to accept, but the truth is my children aren't supposed to think their mom is *hip* and *with it*. For me to be cool defies the natural order of things. That's just the way it's supposed to be. Vinegar and water don't mix. Red will never be blue. A box of See's Candies Nuts and Chews isn't a fat-free food. Mom doesn't equal cool. Those two words go together like spaghetti and sardines. Traffic and relaxation. Seattle and sunshine.

I've decided that there's a perfectly good explanation for this. It's called the mom force. It starts the moment you find out that you're pregnant. It's cemented when you hold your baby. You fall in love with your children. From then on, your only goal is to make them happy and keep them safe. Rolling backpacks, corduroy jackets, and tuna casserole aside, moms just want to see their children enjoying life. Can we help it if that can only be achieved through meddling, embarrassment, and inconvenience?

Now when I think of *low-driving* or *booty-shaking*, I don't cringe in embarrassment. I know who was the coolest of cool; who put the awe in awesome. It's the same woman who wouldn't let me shave my legs until eighth grade and never let me do something just because Liz was allowed to. And I'm grateful that she passed the mom force on to me.

Momisms: A Mother's Words of Advice

My sons will never be mothers. They'll never know firsthand the joys of morning sickness, labor, and delivery. Hopefully, one day they will become parents, but the closest they'll get is to be a dad. And in my world, fatherhood is light years away from motherhood.

Sure, dads teach their children neat stuff like how to hit a ball off a tee, draw to an inside straight, or burp out the National Anthem. But it's mom who imparts the meaningful wisdom, the stuff that changes lives. Moms do more than teach you how to sew on a button or make a hard-boiled egg. Our advice is a mixture of the practical (check for TP *before* you sit down), the emotional (laugh some every day) and the spiritual (what goes around, comes around).

I didn't embrace this role as the family sage. It just came with the territory; this mammoth task of offering insight, common sense, and real-world perspective to my sons. To share the knowledge I've garnered over the past few decades. This is a lifelong project and I realize that a lot of what I have to say isn't original, new, or high-tech. With my advice and $3.75 they could get a *grande mocha* at the mall. In fact, some of my most useful nuggets of enlightenment are borrowed, recycled, or stolen directly from my mom, Florence.

Nevertheless, as the days unfold, I continue to reveal my own brand of "momisms" to Shawn, Jake and

Seth, when I think they're listening—however, frequently they're not. That's usually when I'll hear my mom's voice coming from my mouth. *"Never give up. Don't waste anything. This, too, will pass. You get less wrinkles if you smile."*

I think I've come up with a few of my own gems— words my sons will sagely repeat in years to come, as they become adults, get married, and parent my grandchildren. Here are some of my favorites, offered in no particular order; strategies that help me keep priorities straight in the midst of chaos, confusion, and what we commonly call daily life. Borrow, rewrite or purloin what you wish:

Put things back where you found them.

Spend less than you make.

Don't be in a rush to grow up.

Don't be in a rush for your children to grow up.

Smile often.

Listen more than you talk.

Take time for those you love.

Each day is a new chance to discover your life.

Things work out.

Don't be afraid to say: *I love you. Thank you,* and *I'm sorry.*

Pray, pray, and then pray some more.

A new pair of shoes fixes just about anything.

Stay in the moment.

Take out the trash, even if it isn't your turn.

You'll get another chance.

Put the seat down.

Hug someone every day. When you are hugged, hug back.

Put on a pot of tea.

Use a tissue.

Walk the dog.

Grow roses.

It's okay to be bored.

Don't put the empty box back on the shelf.
Pack an extra pair of underwear.
Floss.
Let the other guy go first.
Take care of your friends.
Count to ten. Count to ten again.

My hope is that what I've learned and tried to pass on to my children will enhance their lives in ways that successful careers and money can't. But that's probably wishful thinking. Let's be real: none of us takes Mom's word for it. I didn't. I had to find things out in my own way. I still do. No shortcuts for Claire. And inevitably, when life presents me with another chance to learn a lesson (check the gas tank before you get on the freeway), I nod my head and think: *Yeah, Mom told me that. She knew.*

My trio of fellas is wandering down their own "I-gotta-learn-it-myself" path. They're figuring out the stuff I tried to tell them. In the years to come, when they become dads, I hope they'll see the value of what I've shared. The greatest compliment to me would be to see that same head nod. A recognition of that *ah-ha* moment when it all comes together. And they'll think*: Yep, Mom really did know what she was talking about.*

WOMAN WISE

Write That Down!

"We're out of toothpaste," my husband shouts from another room. "Which list do I write that on?"

"The purple one," I reply.

I've learned the best bargains on sundries and non-perishables are at a discount chain. I get fresh fruits and veggies from a health food market and everything else from the neighborhood grocery store. So there are three photocopied lists hanging in my pantry—color-coded, of course.

I can't take full credit for this idea. My long-time friend Arlene unintentionally introduced me to the concept years ago during a lunch break. Peering over my turkey sandwich, I spied her preparing an after-work shopping strategy.

"Is your list pre-printed?" I asked.

She laughed. "Yeah, I got tired of writing the same things over and over, so I typed a list and made copies." She handed me a sample. Dish soap, shampoo, dog food, TP. Arlene's system was simple—checkmark the items that were running low.

I naïvely adopted her blueprint, expecting Nick and my sons to embrace the system. I dreamed that, after taking the last of the something, those living in my house would circle it on the list, sending a clear signal to me to replenish the chocolate syrup, tortilla chips, or mouthwash. It didn't take long for Claire-the-realist to propose a compromise; leave the empty "whatever" on the counter.

Family code for "I took the last one."

Living in the digital age, we're inundated with apps to keep track of groceries and home supplies. Still, I prefer the feel of a pen and the crinkle of paper. I love my smartphone as much as the next gal. I've downloaded a whopping forty-seven apps. At the tap of a fingertip, I can tag a song, play word games, or check the status of my delayed flight. Occasionally I use it to make phone calls.

Apps are convenient and amazing, but I've trusted my reminders to a pencil and a spiral notebook for decades. The time it takes to move a ballpoint pen across the page allows my thoughts to crystallize. Plucking at a keyboard or poking a touch screen isn't the same. Besides, paper's battery never dies and even a dull pencil writes.

I was reminded of the benefits of another kind of wireless communication on a late summer afternoon, when our neighborhood lost power. While I prepared for an expanded version of my monthly book club, an unusual quiet blanketed my house. The gentle buzz of the water cooler silenced. Ice cubes didn't drop in the freezer. No digital readout reminded me there's two hours left to chill the white wine. I learned later that a power line had been inadvertently tripped, leaving hundreds of homes without electricity.

I had limited time to notify the usual group of six— temporarily expanded to about thirty, because a local author wrote that month's selection—that without air conditioning and illumination, the meeting was cancelled. My cell phone didn't connect. No internet access, either. Twitter worked for a while, but I knew my group of friends wouldn't be checking my tweets. I could alert those within walking distance by knocking on doors, but shoe leather wouldn't work for the friends who lived farther away. Fortunately, mounted on my kitchen wall was an operating telephone. I dialed a few other traditionalists who still used landlines and asked them to spread the word.

The hot weather made staying inside uncomfortable, so while Seth barbecued already defrosting hamburgers, Nick and Jake dragged a couple tables and chairs to the driveway. Neighbors, rolling coolers filled with ice and carrying goodies originally intended for book clubbers, joined us for an unplugged evening. Conversations flowed and it was hours before the glow of candles dotting the tables faded and flashlights began to dim.

An accidental blackout turned into an impromptu block party for adults, teenagers, and kids who happen to live side-by-side. We savored this unscheduled break from laundry, homework, and economic woes. There was no fretting about what dish to bring or what clothes to wear and plenty of the time to enjoy life off the grid.

That night's blackout was caused by human error, but I'm proposing a planned reenactment this summer. An annual "lights out" night to relax under a star-dusted sky with neighbors and friends. We can switch off, power down, and unplug everything—except the fridge. I'll need matches, candles, and flashlight batteries.

Better write that down on my yellow shopping list.

Reeling in the Deals

The saying goes: It's okay to be thrifty, but not cool to be cheap. It's a delicate distinction to draw for this daughter of a single mother who didn't buy anything unless it was on sale or she had a coupon for it. Glorious was my mom's smile on those rare occasions when she managed to get both ends of the deal working—on sale *and* with a coupon. The ride home from the store was happy for a then-second-grade girl who may have scored new Barbie clothes, Scooter Pies for her lunch pail, or a shiny pair of black patent-leather shoes.

Unlike their mother, my sons never spent an afternoon at our kitchen table, painstakingly gluing green S&H trading stamps into pages of books, only to learn that you're a few pages short of redeeming them for a toaster or a Teflon frying pan. Shawn, Jake, and Seth haven't witnessed gas wars where station attendants pump your gas, clean your windshield, and give you a juice glass with every fill-up. None of my trio ever fished out a free dishtowel from inside a box of laundry detergent.

My guys have seen other thrift-minded routines, though. They've watched their mom covet a dollar-off coupon, look for the bonus box of ten granola bars for the price of eight, and scour the shelves searching for the shampoo bottle that promises twenty-percent more. They understand the economic wisdom of a buy-one, get-one free. There may be no such thing as a free lunch, but they've dined using a $5.99 meal-deal coupon.

In between watching Sunday morning football games, my sons have observed me peel off savings promotions attached to the newspaper's front page and clip coupons from the inserts. The slips of paper, representing potential money in my pocket, are filed by date and category in my teal-colored coupon caddy. Along with my store loyalty card, offers on deodorant, tortilla chips, and dish soap are ready to be cashed in on the next shopping trip.

My kids know to rummage through the coupon drawer located in the entryway table first before spending their money on bowling, a pizza, or a car wash. My husband Nick combs through odd-sized bits of paper I've stored helter-skelter, in search of golf, fishing, or dry-cleaning discounts. There's disappointment if the prized coupon has expired.

Happily, saving money never goes out of style even if the methods for reeling in the deals have changed. I proudly carry on the frugal heritage instilled in my youth, incorporating technology that has enhanced my efforts to save a few bucks. Some supermarkets download discounts right onto your membership card, eliminating the need to clip coupons. I take advantage of deep discounts offered by Groupon.com or other daily deal sites and before I place an online order, I check first to see if there's a percentage-off promo code or free shipping. They have taken the scissors out of my hands, but still put the savings in my purse.

Being thrifty means more than gathering dollars and cents in a check register. It's a challenge that, when conquered, frees me to be generous and—once in a while—even extravagant. When I'm not paying full price for a tube of mascara, a pot roast, or a tune-up, I divert those funds into more meaningful uses. Instead of purchasing products, I have the freedom to spend my time and treasure on memories—a movie date with my husband, a girls' night out (probably a wind-down Wednesday with half-off beverages and appetizers) or a much-needed family getaway weekend.

There's evidence that my bargain-minded values may have taken root in the next generation. Seth, my away-at-college son, called recently to brag about saving fifty dollars on internet installation. In the next breath, he told me about last night's dinner: two-for-the-price-of-one frozen pizzas. Now, that deal would make any mom proud.

A New Wrinkle

Life isn't fair. It's taken me awhile to accept this reality. I've always had my suspicions though, starting when I was six and my brand-new Slinky got a kink in it. But now I have verifiable proof. This morning as I washed my face with anti-aging cleanser, I discovered fresh wrinkles framing the sides of my smile like brackets. No surprises there. What I find unjust is that right below these newborn laugh lines, nature gifted me with a zit. Guess the joke's on me, since I mistakenly believed that once you became old enough to earn wrinkles, your face should be a pimple-free zone. One or the other, I say, but not both. Acne and crow's-feet shouldn't live in perfect harmony.

Clothing designers are messing with me, too. Earlier this month I scoured the stores looking for a bargain-priced party dress. The clearance racks are full of size fours and sixes and eights. Where are the tens, the twelves, the fourteens? Haven't the garment manufacturers figured out there are more of us wearing double digits than gals who can enumerate their clothing size barely using the fingers of both hands?

Calories don't play fair, either. Even when I try to eat healthier, I don't. In my ongoing quest to get skinny, I grabbed a bag of trail mix instead of nibbling on some sugar cookies. The next day I bragged about my improved eating choice to my perfectly fit friend Joni. She laughed. "You'd be better off just eating a handful of M&Ms." I didn't want to believe her, but when I got home, I checked the nutrition facts on the trail mix bag. Joni was right. Excuse me if I sound like a sorehead, but who wants to live in a world where a cup of raisins has seven times as many calories as a bunch of grapes? Who decided that four ounces of tofu has 88 calories while a two-ounce Snickers bar weighs in at 271?

And one more gripe. Why do things break in bunches? In the past ten days, my computer monitor died, my son Seth's entire computer system gave up the ghost, my car battery decided it didn't need to perform any longer, and the icemaker in our barely two-year-old refrigerator developed a constant drip. The topper was two days ago when Nick walked into the kitchen and—with his teeth chattering—asked who turned off the hot water. Alas, our ten-year-old water heater with a nine-year warranty had delivered its last gallon of hot water the night before.

Normally, I'm a glass-half-full kind of girl. I grew up hearing my mom sing along as Bing Crosby belted out "Blue Skies." When my toast lands butter-side down, I brush it off, grateful to have something to eat. Recently though, I find myself tallying up life's many inconveniences instead of reveling in its abundant godsends.

It's a good thing that Thanksgiving and Christmas are just around the corner, because tucked in alongside the hectic hustle and bustle of the season is an annual reminder to pay attention to life's important moments. The holidays gently inspire me to stop being the gal standing in line at the complaint department and spend my time breathing in the sweet, refreshing air of gratitude.

I can quickly list my grumbles in a less-than-eight-hundred-word essay. Thankfully, recounting my life's blessings would take pages and pages of effort. Where do I start? A wonderful childhood. My loving husband. Three healthy and handsome sons. My sisters and brothers who love me in spite of my quirky habits. Long-time friends who—under no genetic obligation—continue to make time for me.

There are many simple, yet sustaining delights— cozy fires, a warm cup of tea, coconut cake, the memory of my mom's voice. My vow is to keep the holiday spirit alive in the coming months and pay better attention to the ever-expanding list of these priceless treasures.

No doubt I'll backslide a time or two—especially around April or July—when the washing machine develops a grinding noise, the minivan gets a flat, and a newly sprouted blemish finds companionship near a brand-new laugh line.

What's Your Rush?

It happened again today. I was late meeting a friend for coffee. As I drove around the parking lot searching for a spot, I caught a glimpse of her sitting at the sidewalk café. Not wasting time waiting for me to show up, she was cleaning out her purse. I apologized for my tardiness as she gave me a hug. "It's no big deal," Margaret said, letting me off the hook. "I've been wanting to clean my purse for a while anyway, but I never could find the time."

The frustrating thing is, I shouldn't have been late in the first place. I was ready to walk out the door fifteen minutes early. But since I had extra time, I tossed a load in the washing machine and wrote an overdue thank-you note.

Presto, now I was running behind.

I start out on time, but for some reason, being early often makes me late. It's like my day is ten minutes shorter than everyone else's. The truth is, being a chronic multitasker (aka woman/mother) has impaired my time-management skills. Even though I've adopted "be in the moment" as my personal mantra, often my actions are focused on reaching the destination instead of enjoying the journey.

My sons don't classify me as a woman-in-constant-motion, even though they're the benefactors of my never-waste-a-moment mentality. To them, I move about as fast as, well, a mom. So several weeks ago when I got pulled over for speeding, they were shocked. In fact, since my speedometer rarely hits sixty, the boys agreed that my car must have been the only one the officer could catch. At the time, my mind was on where I was headed; not how fast I was getting there. Luckily, the patrolman let me off with a stern warning. Maybe I reminded him of his own mother.

I blame my scheduling shortcomings on a high regard for the value of time. I'm committed to squeezing every second out of the day as if I'm crushing oranges so every drop lands in the glass. Time is precious and I don't want to waste it. But somehow in my quest to get the most out of every moment, I'm often rushed, segmented, and rarely able to strike a reasonable balance between using time wisely and staying in the moment.

Just a few weeks ago, while opening the afternoon mail, I noticed a long-awaited check for a freelance writing assignment. I opened the envelope, looked at the amount, smiled and then—as any busy woman and mother of three would do—went on to finish a variety of chores. About a half hour later, I realized I had misplaced the check. Panicked, I retraced my steps. Wow, I had done a lot in those thirty minutes—paid some bills, vacuumed the family room, dropped off magazines at the neighbor's house, fed the dogs. Still, I couldn't find the check.

I was discouraged about losing my hard-earned money, but what really bugged me was how much time I'd wasted looking for that envelope. In my haste to get more done, I'd accomplished less and I felt more stressed for my efforts.

About an hour later I found the check, tucked inside a stack of papers filed for a future writing assignment. Then reality hit me. Doing several things at once can cost more time than it saves—and it doesn't do much to strengthen long-standing friendships, either.

I'm told the best way to solve any problem is to acknowledge it and then take small steps to correct it. I already have a few changes in mind to get me on the path of doing less and enjoying it more. For starters, I could replace quick showers with an occasional lingering bubble bath or eat a real breakfast instead of bites of an untoasted Pop-Tart. On days I really want to splurge, I'll read an entire magazine instead of skimming through the pages and ignore that little voice adding items to my "to-do" list.

There's one improvement I'll make the next time Margaret agrees to meet me for coffee. I'll leave the house fifteen minutes early; no checking e-mail or devising last-minute menu plans. This time she'll find me sitting at the café table with nothing more to do than sip a warm, chocolate-y mocha, happily awaiting her arrival.

Friendships Across the Ages

A plaque hanging above my desk reads: *A good friend forgives your faults. A loving friend doesn't see any.* Carole, my best friend since ninth grade, gave it to me after we graduated from college. Even though we were both high school freshmen, Carole was a year and seven months older. (Mom snuck this mid-December birthday baby into kindergarten a tad early.) We shared a first-floor locker, worried about who'd ask us to the prom, and found our first job at the same self-serve shoe store. Years later, we were in each other's weddings.

To kids and teenagers, age differences of months up to a couple years seem huge. Being friends with Carole was the first time I stepped out of the traditional friendship age range. When I was eight, my classmates were eight years old, too. We third graders wouldn't dream of hanging out with the sixth graders. They were three whole years older. Every girl in my troop standing in front of the grocery store selling Thin Mints was pretty close to my age, too, give or take a month or so.

My junior-high science lab partner Lynn was twelve to my twelve-and-a-half. I proudly added *and-a-half,* thinking it made me sound older. I'd never do that nowadays. If someone asks how old I am, I smile and say thirty-forty-fifty-something. Once you've blown out twenty-nine candles on your birthday cake, you find yourself effortlessly substituting the word *something* for *and-a-half.*

As Carole and I moved into our thirties, that ocean of nineteen months trickled into a stream. I'd grown past letting a driver's license birthdate dictate the width and depth of any friendship pool. No longer limited to scouts working on outdoor cooking badges or classmates in fourth period history, my world of potential gal pals expanded.

This gift of age-blindness slipped seamlessly into my life, enticing me to scoop up friends of all ages and pour them into my social kaleidoscope. In both of my book clubs, I think I'm one of the youngest. For certain I'm the oldest of the seven in my writers' group. With my long-time work friends, Laura, Elaine, Jackie, and Arlene (lovingly known as the Zoo Gals), I'm smack-dab in the middle. I have no idea where I fit in chronologically with the varsity football decoration moms, my yoga friends, the soccer moms, or my husband Nick's personal favorite—the Tuesday Night Chick Flick movie gang. What I do know is, I cherish these diverse rings of friendship radiating through time and generational barriers.

I'm lucky enough to be friends with women who have kids in first grade and moms who stood shoulder-to-shoulder with me as we watched our children graduate high school. Many of these gals are my age. Some were born the year I graduated high school. Some have kids the same age as mine. A couple of them have children my age.

The more friends I embrace, the more this vibrant rainbow of wisdom, common sense, and laughter enriches and nourishes me. Many of us remember black-and-white TV, ten-cent phone calls and life before e-mail. For a few of the younger ones, Bush/Kerry was the first presidential election they voted in. They only know self-serve gas stations and a postage stamp has never cost under thirty cents. Who cares? True friendship trumps accumulated days on a calendar.

In this spectrum of sisterhood, sometimes it's me offering nuggets of knowledge, insight, and experience to waiting ears. But more often than not, in between sips of hot tea or a cabernet, I'm the sponge soaking in every scrap of advice and savoring every nuance of humor. In our camaraderie, no topic is off limits. No favor too great to ask. No victory too small to celebrate. No hug left unreturned.

I owe my unabashed disregard for age-defining boundaries to Carole, who crossed the line with me. I'm living proof that it's wiser, healthier, and way more fun to tally friends instead of years. You can be sure at my next birthday party—in between licking chocolate icing off my fingertips—I'll be counting those folks waiting for a slice of cake instead of the number of candles I blew out.

Friendless on Facebook

This was a moment to savor—collecting on a lunch bet from my long-time friend Tony. With the jubilance of Queen's "We Are the Champions" playing in my mind, I dipped my hosted onion ring into a tasty pool of ranch dressing. During our nine-year history of pitting our baseball or football teams against one another, this was one of my few victories. My triumphant mood, though, was quickly erased like yesterday's box scores. Replacing it was the awkward feelings of a skinny fifth-grade girl standing on the volleyball court anxiously waiting to be picked.

The waitress had just refilled our ice teas when Tony said, "I looked you up on Facebook." In between bites of his cheeseburger, he added, "You have one friend."

Choking down my last bit of onion ring, I hurried to explain that I'd joined to contact a friend I'd lost touch with. Outwardly I blamed Vicki, my one and only FB friend, for the embarrassment.

Inwardly, those four simple words—*you have one friend*—sat on my stomach like an expanding weight, daring me to defend my popularity. Savvy internet users thought that my lifetime of experiences had yielded one lone friend. An off-the-cuff observation reduced me from a confident wife and mother to an insecure ten-year-old whose happiness was measured by the width of her circle of friends.

I thought it was pretty amazing that I had any presence on this phenomenon of a social-networking site. I'd heard of Facebook. My sons had MySpace pages, but until lunch that day, I never saw the value of getting involved. Tony's cavalier comment had launched me headfirst into the intricacies of online communities.

For days I surfed the web, clicking, searching, and tinkering my way through the sites. Before I knew it, I was writing on Tony's wall, re-tweeting posts on Twitter and uploading links. I also learned that the reasons people join these sites are as varied as the folks themselves. After sending out some friend requests and joining the SDSU alumni group, I couldn't help but wonder if anyone else had hitched up to quell their elementary school ghosts.

In my urgency to prove that I was a likeable sort, I'd stumbled on an instantaneous way to stay connected. Years ago I swapped the daily workplace security for the freedoms of being a stay-at-home writer. With that change came the realization that I missed my coworkers and our daily impromptu discussions about last night's episode of *24* or what movie isn't worth the ten-bucks-plus-popcorn ticket. The chats about kids, cars, and diets that I took for granted as part of my workday now came to me via an anytime cyberspace-coffee break. I got status updates from my colleagues, my cousins, and everyone else in between. This morning I learned *25 Random Things* about Fran, my god-sister in Pittsburgh; where Jane, my gal pal in St. Louis, went for her birthday dinner; and how many points my ten-year-old nephew Zach scored during his basketball game in Sacramento.

Usually my posts are innocuous—a home-decorating victory, a recent challenge of being a mom, a book recommendation. But last month, when our family made the difficult decision to put our sickly sixteen-year-old spaniel mix down, I turned to Facebook. I wanted to express my grief and let everyone know how special this soccer-playing dog was to us. Within moments I had posted a farewell to Max—photos and all. Seconds later and for the next several days, condolences and comfort streamed electronically into my home.

Courtesy of my broadband connection, job changes, geography, or jammed schedules aren't hurdles to staying in touch with people who—in big or small ways—have enriched my life. They're now a part of my day and I have a new place—and an avatar—in theirs.

At last check, my Facebook friends' list has grown to eighty-six. I'm following fifty-four people on Twitter and about seventy folks follow @ClaireFlaire. I have a blog. And I have Tony, my second FB friend, to thank. Who knew that winning a hamburger could be so rewarding?

Stuck on Sticky Notes

People often ask: *Where do you get ideas for your essays?* Well, this one came to me during the cooldown after my step class. In between calling out commands to stretch our calf muscles, our young instructor, Sabra, lamented that she's starting to forget things. "I'm now dependent on sticky notes to keep my life in order," she groaned as we relaxed the biceps in our upper arms. She feared her gray matter was having too many gray moments.

Nervous laughter swept through the class of twenty, all over the age of forty-something. In between exhales, I smiled and gave her a knowing nod. *I've survived for years thanks to sticky notes, to-do lists and e-mail reminders.* My motto: The shortest pencil is better than the longest memory.

I've made peace with having to write everything down. In fact, I wrote down the idea for this column as soon as I got home from class, or I would have forgotten. Many in my circle of girlfriends share this malady. We've discovered that as life gets busier, it's harder and harder to remember simple things. We racked our brains to recall the name of an actor we saw in a movie last night. Wondered if we left the milk on the counter. We forgot where we put car keys, cell phones, and sometimes for a moment or two, even our kids.

I used to fret about losing my memory, but I don't any more. With age-earned wisdom, I liken sporadic forgetfulness to a baseball catcher's overload. With a job, a husband, kids, dogs, and a book club, there are simply too many balls to snatch. The less urgent stuff—buying stamps, taking out the trash, or fertilizing the roses—occasionally drops out of my mitt. That's not a sign that dementia is my next stop on the train ride of life.

There's no shame in relying on a system—even if it's made up of colorful scraps of paper—to help you remember to turn off the flatiron or pick up poster board at the drug store. There are lots of mornings I jot down a to-do list before I've gotten out of bed. I stash a pad and pencil in my nightstand drawer for that reason. Random notes to remind me to: e-mail Cathy about a book I just finished; figure out what movie theaters are near Houston before I buy a gift card for my nephew; or pull the pot roast out of the freezer so we can eat before eight tonight.

So what if I can't remember the name of Dan Brown's newest book (*Origin*) or the collective term for a group of turtles (a dole). I've already apologized to my teammates for our third-place finish in last month's trivia challenge. I should have remembered the book title. I don't think I ever knew the turtle term, though.

For decades, my head's CPU has been bombarded with information. My computer-like brain is always on the job, processing data gathered from my thousands of days on this earth. When I was twelve, it was so much easier. I barely had a decade of life under my belt. Twelve years of fact and fiction to keep straight. Maybe three contemporary US presidents and four Beatles to remember. There was lots of room in my head to memorize state capitals, multiplication tables, and words for a spelling test. Homework was my brainteaser. If there was something important I needed to do, my mom reminded me. Back then I had maybe fifty people in my life, including schoolmates, aunts, uncles, and TV characters. Nowadays, more folks than that follow me on Twitter.

As the years pile up, so does the minutia. Names, places, computer programs, all vying for a spot in the mind's filing cabinet. It's an ongoing battle to determine what's worth remembering, what can be retrieved by a Google search, and what to delete from your cerebral hard drive. No one keeps track of everything. And why would we want to when there are notepads, calendars, and other memory-saving shortcuts at our beck and call?

More power to those of us who've joyfully embraced our yellow and pink sticky notes as a white flag of surrender. We fight back by keeping our minds sharp and our pencils sharper.

There was one more thing I was going to add, but I forgot what it was.

Guess I should have written it down.

That's A Twist

Standing on my yoga mat, I step my legs about three feet apart and point my right foot forward. My arms form a T and I rotate from my waist, sending my left hand in the air and my right hand sliding down my left leg toward my foot. Patricia, our yoga teacher, encourages us to "breathe deeply."

Some twenty minutes earlier, I'd unrolled my mat in line next to Virginia, Marisol, and Beatriz, my yoga pals. There's a bunch of us who weave this bit of "me-time" into our routine. About thirty men and women relying on these bends, twists, and stretches to help unite mind, body, and spirit.

As I take a slow inhalation and hold this twisted triangle pose, my thoughts page back to eighth grade. My classmate Maggie's 13th birthday party. *If I had been practicing yoga then, I would have won that game of Twister, instead of toppling over after her mom called out: "Right hand on blue. Left foot on green."*

Since junior high, I've learned a lot about mental and physical adaptability. The fact that I'm the mother of three sons has contributed greatly. But recently I credit my enhanced limberness and awakened inner peace to yoga. Three mornings a week—for a blessed seventy-five minutes—my world stops as I stand tall in mountain pose and breathe from my belly.

Before I started practicing yoga, my body (and spirit) sent out steady, achy complaints. These pain-racked signals culminated in an all-out demand for me to learn how to relax my soul and quiet my mind. One undeniable yoga signpost came during lunch with my good friend Sue. After our usual updates about kids, husbands and careers, our girl talk took a more personal tilt: "So what are you doing for yourself these days?" she asked in between bites of our shared tiramisu.

I was glad she asked. As a result of a recent scare with high blood pressure, I had become a self-proclaimed expert about benefits of meditation. And with the over-the-top enthusiasm characteristic of the newly converted, I launched into a PowerPoint-worthy presentation on the pluses of quiet contemplation.

Sue smiled and then asked, "Have you ever considered yoga?" After another bite of dessert, she added tentatively, "You know you are, uh, wound a bit tight sometimes."

I knew she wasn't referring to the snug spirals of my naturally curly hair. In her own understated way, Sue was suggesting that—like lots of women—I tended to overreact to everyday dilemmas. I was guilty of attacking each mini-drama as the next hill to die on. And maybe, just maybe, my current coping style wasn't the sanest way to live if I wanted to be around to see my grandkids.

As an eighth grader, I didn't realize that playing a "game that ties you up in knots" was a peek into the future. At thirteen, how could I know that pretty much everything in life takes agility—college, relationships, children, careers. We have to find balance, but no one tells you how you lost it or where to look for it once you've discovered it's missing. So it's no wonder that when we take on too much, we topple over. I am a loving partner (left foot on yellow) and a good mother (right foot on blue). I hold down a job (left hand on red), care for an aging parent (right foot on green) and try to find a smidgen of time for myself (right hand on blue).

Except for an occasional kid's birthday party, my Twister days are behind me. These days I find balance in my wobbly attempts to stand in tree pose. I concentrate on being still on the inside so that later, when one of life's inevitable twists or turns arises, I can stay calm on the outside.

Still standing in revolved triangle, Patricia's soft voice encourages the class to breathe more deeply. "Open up your chest by turning a little more toward the back of the room." My thoughts interrupt: *What's for dinner? Did I unplug the iron? I wonder if the check hit the bank yet. Boy, I'd love a piece of cake.* Yoga has improved my range of motion, but I'm still working on the "letting-go-of-my-thoughts" part of this restorative discipline.

With encouragement from yogis like Patricia, and thanks to Sue, I'm gradually getting it. During these few minutes, worries about food, kids, and money float through my mind like bubbles in the breeze. I remind myself that I have the rest of the day to figure out what to get my niece for her birthday.

But for now, while I'm in class, I work on staying in the moment. Patricia, like Maggie's mom did decades ago, calls out a new pose—right foot and right hand on green, left foot and left hand on blue. I slowly position myself into downward-facing dog and breathe deeply.

More Payne, More Gain

I used to be a couch potato, hoping that fitness was just a fad. Convinced that I looked good in double-digit jeans, I became expert at finding clothes labeled *relaxed fit, tummy control* and *instantly slimming.* By the end of each day, my energy was so low that I nodded off during *Jeopardy.*

Things started turning around, though, after my doctor made it clear that maintaining my current *out-of-shape* shape wasn't a viable health strategy. During my annual checkup, I listened as he lectured about the importance of a regular fitness plan. And, he said, it had to include weight-bearing exercises to strengthen my bones. My gelatinous thighs and jiggly underarms moved in agreement. I got the message; this PE delinquent needed to get serious about exercise.

A researcher by profession, I'd toyed with the concept of exercising before. I talked to friends, gathered flyers, read brochures, and considered class schedules. Pinned on my bulletin board was a two-year-old e-mail reply from the local Y to my inquiry about yoga classes.

When I got home after my checkup, I pulled out my research and sifted through the many choices, times and locations. My eyes were drawn to: **Step and Sculpt:** This fun and high-energy class combines easy-to-follow step aerobics with strength conditioning. Perfect to slim and tone all over. P. Payne, instructor.

I thought about the last time I'd worked out on a step, more than a decade ago. I had more energy, my clothes fit better and I felt good about myself. My now-high school-age son, Seth, was attending a tiny tots program, laptops were where you put your napkin, and no one I knew got their coffee from a *barista.*

This twice-a-week step aerobics class at City Recreation Center had everything I needed, and it was only fifty-five minutes long. It seemed like a good way to get back on the road to fitness. Out of excuses, I sucked in my stomach, grabbed my sneakers and water bottle, crossed my fingers and signed up.

On the first day of class, I left my half-finished mocha and the morning newspaper unread to get there on time. Still not sure that I'd made the right decision, I secured a spot in the back of the room, near the door for a quick escape. After a few warm-up stretches, I blended in—just another gal in a group of twenty fifty-somethings, trying to remember her right foot from her left. The music boomed hits from the nineties. Patricia, our instructor, yelled out cues: *March Right, Alternate Hamstring Curl, "L Step."* It took a few minutes, but the choreography came back to me. I was stepping, kicking, and lifting in lockstep with everyone else; firing up muscles that hadn't been used this century. My heart rate quickened with every *Grapevine to the Right* and *Three-knee Repeater* she commanded.

Weeks went by. We gals—sweating our way through whatever exercise-set-to-music routine this physical-fitness powder keg threw at us—bonded in our common goal. Patricia showed no mercy to our muscles. Triceps, biceps, abs, quads, it didn't matter. She angered them all. And then, after forty minutes of aerobics, the real workout began. She brought out exercise balls, resistance bands and hand weights; medieval torture devices designed to push us to the next level. Lunges, curls, crunches, push-ups—she mastered them all and for some crazy reason, she thought we could, too.

Patricia motivated, challenged, and cajoled each of us to work harder. So it wasn't surprising that, after several weeks, I saw progress—definition returned to my upper arms, my thighs didn't keep moving after the rest of me had stopped and I'd overcome my need for an afternoon nap. Excited to share my good news, I stayed after class. I wanted Patricia to know that it was her sincere words of encouragement that kept me off the couch and on the gym floor.

"I'm getting a lot from your class," I said, my quads still burning after a particularly strenuous set of squats. "After the first couple of classes, I didn't know if I'd make it or not. But I'm glad I hung in there. I feel stronger and things aren't as jiggly as they were."

She smiled. "I knew you could do it. Just keep it up and you'll be back in shape by summer."

I nodded, not wanting to entertain the thought of swimsuits just yet. "But I have to confess that I almost didn't sign up for your class. I was worried about taking an aerobics class instructed by someone named Payne," I said, chuckling at my own joke.

She stuffed her towel in her workout bag and turned back to me. "Good thing you didn't know that my maiden name is Moore."

Walk It Off

It started with nibbling on leftover Halloween candy; my two months of overindulgence. Almond-cranberry stuffing, artichoke dip and a two-pound box of See's candy (nuts and chews) combined forces to put me where I am today...toting those infamous seven pounds that many of us are supposed to gain during the holiday season.

I can't say I didn't enjoy myself during the eight weeks of tasting the fruits of the holidays—or at least the fruit *flavors* of the holidays. Even though I wasn't curling up with a bowl of strawberries or a plate of celery, I did learn a few things. For example, did you know that there are 1,050 fat-free calories in a 9.5-oz box of Hot Tamales? Me neither. I found out the hard way when my usually forgiving relaxed-fit jeans refused to zip up and the numbers on my digital scale boldly climbed to where they've never gone before.

The good news is that my heavy weight predicament is temporary. I believe I can alter the stretch of my waistline by going back to my tried-and-true weight-maintenance techniques. That, and I'd have to knock off eating snickerdoodles for breakfast. All it will take is trading that slice of French apple pie for an apple, skipping the late-night hot toddy and getting back to my two-mile walking routine. No problem. My brain understands. I just have to convince the rest of my body.

I dig out my sneakers from the back of the closet. They are hiding under a pair of fuzzy reindeer slippers and my rhinestone-studded black satin heels. With a couple swipes of a dust cloth, they're ready to go.

I grab my iPod, a house key, my cell phone, and head for the door. Earbud in each ear, I take a deep breath and set out on a familiar loop around my neighborhood; past the 7-Eleven, through the jogging trail, around the middle school, and back up the hill toward home.

Within a few steps, my pace slips easily into sync with Chaka Kahn singing, "I'm Every Woman." Her voice gives me a mantra of encouragement. I lengthen my stride. McFadden and Whitehead are next on my playlist, booming "Ain't No Stopping Us Now." With every step I can feel the calories burn. *Ah, there goes that extra helping of green bean casserole...*

Aretha belts out some "R-E-S-P-E-C-T." I nod to another walker headed in the opposite direction. Steppenwolf's "Born to Be Wild," Natasha Bedingfield's "Unwritten," and Chic's "Good Times" energize my trek. For a moment, I consider breaking into a jog. I can feel the healthy benefits of this cardiovascular workout. My heart rate is skyrocketing! The pounds are melting off! All those tips I learned from walking guru Leslie Sansone are paying off!

I keep the pace up for another song or two and then reality sets in. I'm taking deeper breaths. My calf muscles are screaming. My sneakers feel tight. My mouth is dry and my thighs are burning. *Why didn't I push myself away from the table before seconds were served?* I curse the sweet treats I ate over the holidays. Denise's baklava, Sue's fruitcake, and Sadye's pistachio nut roll aren't worth the roll they've added to my waist.

My vision of fitting into my skinny jeans fades. I daydream of retreating back to my couch potato state. *What was I thinking? I haven't exercised since TV's fall season premiere week.* My legs start to betray me. Annoyed with my shoddy fitness level, I switch my playlist to slower songs; Fontella Bass's "Rescue Me" and "Born to Lose" by Ray Charles. My gait slows to a canter and then a stroll. As I meander past house after house, longing to be home, I notice my heart rate bottom out. The powerful, energizing *PUMP-PUMP-PUMP* I felt pounding in my chest is reduced to a scant *thump-thump-thump.* I dialed Seth, to see if he'll pick me up. But before I push *send*, I re-think the idea. I'll never hear the end of having to be driven home when I was less than five blocks away—even if they're all uphill.

Louis Armstrong's "Wonderful World" slowly spurs me on. I find new inspiration. I smile at seeing the street sign signaling that my block is just moments away. I switch my player to hear Gloria Gaynor proclaim, "I Will Survive" and make the final turn toward my cul-de-sac.

Persistence pays off. I've won the battle over my sluggish, out-of-shape body. Just two more minutes and I can sit on our brick wall in my front yard and catch my breath.

Later, after slurping down a glass of cold water, I realize that the walk wasn't so bad after all. Being outside in the sunshine, breathing fresh air, and enjoying nature was just what I needed.

A few more outings like this and I'll be back in shape in plenty of time to feast on Valentine's Day chocolates.

Hey, What's Your Name?

It happened again this week. I was in the cereal aisle, lost in a mental debate about the nutritional merits of Fruity Pebbles vs. Trix. That's why I didn't see it—or rather, him—coming. It wouldn't have mattered. I wasn't prepared.

"Hey Claire. How's Nick?" a deep voice spoke.

Peering up from the box panels, I see a smile from a man pushing his half-full cart toward me. *He looks familiar*, I think. *I know him, but from where?* He clearly recognizes me.

"Oh, hey," I answer, trying to get my mind working. *Who is this guy?* I'm pretty sure he's one of the husbands who lives on the far end of the cul-de-sac. Is it Tom or Greg? I always get those two mixed up. No wonder. I talk to them twice a year—at the July block party and the neighborhood Christmas get-together. I've lived in the same house for a long time. I should remember this guy.

I keep eye contact, nodding and smiling. I'm really waiting for a hint to solve the mystery. Time passes slowly when you can't remember someone's name and he's said yours like he was there the day you were christened. Eventually my neighbor of a decade or more says: "…loved the new color you painted your house. Much better than the light blue. Millie thinks we need to repaint ours. Who did you use?"

Millie. Yes, that's it. She's married to Tom.

I breathe a sigh, inwardly my heart cheers. "Nick picked that sandy brown color with dark blue trim," I reply. My smile relaxes and I fight the urge to pump my fist in the air, and shout *yeah!* Instead I say: "I'll have him call you, Tom, with the painter's phone number."

Three aisles later, I'm choosing a bunch of bananas when I spot another familiar face. I recognize the smile, but I don't recall her name. Of course, she greets me with a boisterous: "Claire! Hi, how have you been?"

"Oh, hey," I shout with a little too much exuberance in my voice, revealing—at least to myself—that I have no idea who she is. "It's great to see you," I say, stalling for time. I'm hoping that she'll drop a clue as to how we are acquainted. We exchange pleasantries before she starts walking away. Over her shoulder, she says, "Tell your husband we said hi. Jimmy still talks about Coach Nick and the fun he had playing T-ball on the Green Hornets."

Now I remember, but it's too late. She's Madeline and we spent hours together sitting in the Little League bleachers. A friendship forged through cheering on six-year-olds as they attempted to belt one into left field. How could I have forgotten?

It's frustrating when you run into acquaintances or neighbors on unfamiliar turf. You're seeing them out of context—not where you're accustomed to meet. I'd know Madeline if we were in line at the baseball field's snack bar, or Tom if he was walking his dog on our block. But while I'm pushing a shopping cart past the instant oatmeal or thumping cantaloupe in the produce section, I'm at a disadvantage. I recognize the face, but I'm often left grasping for a thread to help me piece together our history.

It's a sincere courtesy to remember someone's name. Our name is our calling card, it's who we are, a concrete sign of our individuality. I've been on both sides of this name-calling dilemma. I know I'm not the only one guilty of forgetting a name; or worse yet, using the wrong name. I've endured being called Connie, Chris, and Cecelia. It hurt my ego a little, so I try to not repeat the *faux pas*.

The odds of committing this social blunder increase with age and all the interactions that are simply a part of living. Becoming a parent ups the ante considerably. In my case, add in three kids (Shawn, Jake, Seth) multiply that by their activities (soccer, basketball, scouting) and then mix in the number of years they've done those things. The result is a long list of prospects, many more than my meager brain can keep straight. I find myself mentally scanning a roll call of possibilities: Church? No. PTA? Perhaps. The bank? Probably not. Yoga class? Nope. I've got it. She's our letter carrier. But by the time I've figured out the connection, the person has moved on, probably convinced that I'm scatterbrained.

I stayed in the produce section for several minutes after Madeline walked away. I was afraid that the dog groomer, the dentist, or the paperboy was waiting for me near the deli counter. I could use these meetings as an opportunity to do better.

Or, if I were smart, I'd avoid the entire scenario by simply changing where I shop. Twenty or twenty-five miles from home should be a safe distance.

New and Improved!

My World of Simple Pleasures

I was born forty-two years after my mother, during a time of innovation, progress, and the Beatles. And although the most important ingredients necessary to be a good mother—love, discipline, patience, faith, and a sense of humor—remain the same, there are many reasons I'm glad that I got to be a mom in this day and age instead of in the 1960s. There are inventions, newfangled ideas, and discoveries that streamline my life in ways my mother would have never envisioned.

Sure, she lived in astonishing times. Advances like cars, television, Teflon pans, and supermarkets made parenting easier for her than for her own mother. I'm certain my mom marveled at her laundry chute, coal delivery, the five-string clothesline in our backyard, and Tupperware.

But if she were a young mother today, she'd be amazed at the many services, shortcuts, and accommodations we have at our fingertips. Think tanks all over the world are busy creating products to make our tasks easier, our homes cozier, our lives healthier, and our spirits lighter. Maybe they're not major strides in civilization, like finding a cure for polio or traveling across the country by airplane. But these small, simple pleasures bring a smile to my face, a song to my ear, and can reduce the wrinkles around my eyes. I stay on the lookout for them, because if I don't, I might take them for granted.

Little things like dishwashers, surge strips, permanent press, and smudge-proof lipstick impact the quality of my daily life. Improvements, enhancements, and technological advances like these get me through the workweek with minimal wear and tear. Not only do conveniences like these make me look better and feel better; because of them I have time to spare. I can relax, take a walk with my husband, or join my sons in a game of Yahtzee instead of ironing, hanging laundry, or standing in line at the post office.

In many ways it's a tad easier to be a woman in the 21st century than it was in, say, 1807. Here are, in no particular order, some fifty-seven reasons why I'm happy to be living today. I'm sure by tomorrow my list of simple pleasures will expand to include another five or ten items. Every woman has her own favorites to add, if she takes the time to think about it.

> Kleenex with aloe
> Dimmer switches
> Safety car seats
> Squeezable jelly
> Mascara remover
> Google
> Frozen pancakes
> Crock-Pots, Crock-Pot cookbooks, Crock-Pot liners
> Nutrition facts labeling
> Gift registries
> Baby swings and walkers
> Voice mail
> Ceiling fans
> Salad bars
> Disposable diapers
> Maps and GPS on my cell phone
> Playlands at fast-food restaurants

Handheld frothers
Mobile dog groomers
Fast-forward and rewind
Copy and paste
Airport cell phone parking lots
Portable cribs
Toothpaste with flip-top caps
Photocopies
Instant oatmeal
Baby monitors
Carbonless copies
TV remotes with a sleep timer button
Pre-cooked chicken
Wrinkle-resistant shirts
Flight trackers
Caller ID
Daily moisturizer with SPF 30
Heated driver seats
Digital cameras
Flavored coffee creamers
Self-adhesive postage stamps you can order by mail
Friends of the Library used book store
Gift cards
Music playlists
Online shopping
Richard Carlson's *Don't Sweat the Small Stuff*
Relaxed fit jeans
Microwave ovens
Hearing my "Sweet Child of Mine" ringtone when one of my sons calls
Bread makers
Sesame Street
The Weather Channel
Return address labels
Gift receipts
ATMs

Cash back

Book club readers' guides

Extended-wear contact lenses

The craziness, chaos, and demands of life slow down by the end of the day. It's then that I can sit quietly with a cup of Irish Breakfast tea and let my thoughts settle. That's when it hits me—during these few quiet moments when everyone's safely tucked in bed. After all their homework is done and the lunches are packed, I once again realize what I'm most grateful for: the good health and happiness of my family.

But there's also a soft spot in my heart for that pre-grated cheddar cheese in the handy zipper-lock bag that makes taco night a breeze.

BIWM: Before I Was Mom

I have a name and I like it; Claire. From the French for bright and clear. My mother chose it. She searched through baby-naming books. She fought off pressure to use traditional family names to pick this unique one. For all of her hard work, I'll bet she's not happy with the variations it's undergone.

Unlike Elizabeth (Liz, Libby, Beth, etc.) there aren't a lot of diminutives for Claire. The most memorable attempt was Claircy. Fortunately, it never stuck. I think that's why she chose Claire. There is no viable nickname.

However, Mom didn't think it all the way through. She should have suspected, being a mother of four herself, how my name and my identity would change. She knew what happens and she never shared the secret with me.

Now my name frequently includes the word "mom." As in: "the pitcher's mom," "the goalie's mom" and my personal favorite: "Shawn's mom. You know, the mother of the boy Julie has a crush on." Not quite the name bestowed at baptism, and a tough one to fit on my driver's license. During all of these conversations, no one tried to find out my given name.

My friends, on the other hand, have no problem saying my name, no variations included. They call me Claire. Never am I referred to as "that boy's mother." With my girlfriends, my identity is never in question.

Being mom takes precedence over everything else in my life. It's the most important work I do and I do it with love. But I wasn't born a mom. I did have a life before I had my sons. I am a person, who's also a mom. That's who I was before I became Shawn's mom, Jake's mom, and Seth's mom.

With my gal pals, I'm Claire. A person first, a mom second. That's why I need to connect with these ladies regularly—my longtime friends from when we worked together. Who are these women providing support and free therapy at the drop of a hat? Laura, Jackie, Arlene, and Elaine are an e-mail away. From the north end of the county to the south, we jump at the chance to get together. We pick a night, meet in the middle, and catch up on where our lives have taken us since our last gal-pal meeting. Each of us knows the importance of enduring friendships; peers with a history and a commonality of purpose.

Although our careers changed, our friendships remained constant. For those three or four hours every few months, the mom role takes a back seat. And it feels good. I'm among people who don't think my finest talents lie in making a grilled cheese sandwich. To them I'm not the source of the phrase: *Pick up your mess!* They don't think the words *old* and *Claire* go together. Not one of them uses the designation *annoying* when referring to me.

At least not when I can hear it.

Among the five of us, we mother ten kids. That's a lot of schedules to coordinate—kids' games, birthday parties, music lessons, and whatnot. It takes a bit of planning, and it's rare when we all don't make a gathering. We never refer to each other as Michele, Colin, Jason or Bryce's mom, just to name a few.

My friends remember when TV shows were only in black and white. There were maybe three channels, not 300. They grew up making popcorn in a pot on the stove, not in a bag in the microwave. Our term papers didn't include internet references. Caller ID, cell phones, instant messages—all things our parents didn't deal with.

These are my friends. Women in the same place, at the same time, working to raising our sons and daughters as best we can. We know each other as individuals. That's why we enjoy an occasional mocha, unlimited popcorn at the movies, or an outing to the Cheesecake Factory.

Each day as my children grow, I'm reminded of how quickly things change. That's why being mom is always the priority. But on those golden occasions, when I take a few minutes to reconnect with the woman behind the mom, I learn more about being Claire. That's important, too.

If you don't think so, just ask George, Sadye, Paul, and Claire's mom. Her name is Florence.

Shamrocks of Success

I'm not much of a gardener. Trowels, soil, and seeds don't show any special love for me. The successes I've found are few and many seasons between. I do have one small accomplishment that I joyfully point my green thumb to—my planter box of shamrocks. For three years, these green, tri-leafed plants have managed to survive my care. The same can't be said for other plants, flowers, and living things I've overwatered, under-fertilized or didn't sow in moderate sun.

But not my shamrocks. Through thick and thin, rain or shine, these emerald gems greet me each morning. The first time I noticed that their leaves fold together at night, I thought, "Oh no! I've killed another one." But these bits of clover fooled me. Bright and early the next day, their leaves pointed toward the morning sun, like faces lifted to the warmth.

My gardening triumph. My shamrocks.

I relayed my victory, with strains of pride in my voice to Jen, the owner of a neighborhood flower shop. I sought her advice on buying a hearty houseplant when I felt the need to brag a bit about my own green acres. "I grow shamrocks," I boasted. "I bought them three St. Patrick's Days ago and they're still going strong." Jen nodded at me, as I relayed my tale of conquest. There was a pitying look on her face

"What's wrong with shamrocks?" I finally asked, fearing an answer I didn't really want to hear.

"Shamrocks," she counseled, "are weeds. And you have to be careful not to let them get anywhere near your yard or you'll have a real mess on your hands."

Obviously, she had no idea that my husband Nick and I would be thrilled to have something green growing in our yard, *genus weeds* or not. I later learned that oxalis, or wood sorrel, pop up everywhere and are often sold as "shamrocks."

I left her shop with less of a bounce in my walk. My shoulders slumped a bit, weakened by my newfound knowledge of weed-ology. I looked at my shamrock-infested flower box that night when I got home. The shamrocks were no different than they were that morning when I left for work, but my attitude toward them certainly was.

"You're nothing but weeds," I lamented, feeling the full strength of my green thumb turning a walnut shade of brown.

I labored in a gardener's fantasy where I was the queen, only to find out that my success was, in someone else's eyes, quite a failure. My grand world of growing lush plants—well, one lush plant—had been tarnished. In the span of sixty seconds, less than the time it takes to mist your ferns, my victory was reduced to defeat.

The next day, I sat on my front stoop, staring at my clovers of betrayal. There they sat, happily filling my oblong terra-cotta pot. I felt comfort and satisfaction as I admired their strong stalks. They were thriving and as far as I'm concerned, I was the reason. They might be weeds to Jen, but they're foliage to me.

That day I learned that success is a point of view. It's subjective.

Now I acknowledge my achievements wherever I find them. And I've grown into quite the *success detective*, observing the little victories that make up everyday life.

Success is everywhere, just waiting to be discovered. Some recent triumphs: Losing my Christmas weight. Finding a bargain. Seeing the smile of understanding on my son's face as he figures out his math homework. Being there for a friend. Finding the perfect word. Getting that parking spot in the front row.

Spurred on by my prolific shamrocks, I seek other greenery conquests. I now grow African violets–after learning that you must set them in a plate of water to allow their roots to soak up the puddle. My rose bushes flourish nourished with occasional banana skins and fertilizer twice a year. I've expanded my gardening scope to include daffodils. Encouraged by the words of a good friend: "they grow anywhere," I eagerly await the first bloom of the ones I planted last spring. (I checked: daffodils are flowers, not weeds). I am selective about my horticultural successes. I do try to keep a realistic focus on my gardening aspirations, however. The improved health of my rose garden won't merit a hybrid tea rose being named *Claire's Delight*.

As for my shamrocks, in year four, they're still growing strong. They greet me each morning as if to say: "Ah ha, we've fooled them again!" To some accomplished gardeners they may be considered a weed, but to me, all I see is a beautiful plant, thriving under my loving care. That's success.

My Done List

I woke up every morning last year with a mental to-do list taking form in my mind. Before I'd brushed my teeth or smelled the coffee brewing, I already had at least six things rolling around in my thoughts; stuff I needed to get done that day.

Like many women, moms in particular, I usually have several projects going at the same time—watching TV while wrapping presents; making spaghetti and chatting on the phone, filing my nails while waiting at a red light. I'm notorious for working on one thing while contemplating the next. I guess it would be okay to do two or three things at once if I'd gain some time at the end of the day to relax and enjoy. Surprisingly, that extra time never surfaces and I've figured out why. My to-do list never ends.

On the contrary—it's a growing, changing, swelling catalog of work-in-progress.

It's taken me a while, but I've finally realized that my in-box is always going to be full; there's something waiting to be done, no matter how organized and tenacious I am. That's just the way life is. Seth's dirty football jersey is balled up in a corner of the TV room and his game is in an hour; there's a birthday party tomorrow and I haven't gotten a gift; and, of course, I have no idea what's for dinner.

This is why I'm implementing a new system this year. It's the antithesis of the *To-Do List: The Done List.*

I'm following through with my plan even though my son Jake thinks I'm a bit nuts. When I told him about my "done list" concept, he rolled his eyes so far back in his head I am sure he could see where he's been.

Here's how *The Done List* works: I keep track of what I've completed each day. Big checkmarks lining up right along with the *stuff still to do*. Instead of focusing my energies on what I didn't get to—the plants that need watering or the check that still needs to be written—I now see my to-do list as a hand-written record of daily accomplishments. I anticipate watching it transform; crossed off items commingled with the Still-To-Do stuff. Now, each morning I'm not greeted with a fresh, untouched to-do list emphasizing the stuff left undone from the day before. I can revel in what's been done.

This is great motivation for changing my behavior—that and the hope that I can put my third list into action. My *Want-To-Do List*. Here's how I see that list shaping up:

- read a chapter from a Louise Penny book;
- write a chapter in my book;
- make a phone call to a long-time friend;
- drink my tea while it's still hot;
- have a conversation with my husband that doesn't include anything about our sons or NFL football.
- Sit quietly for fifteen minutes; pray.

As a young girl, I remember my mother saying: "The hurrier I go, the behinder I get." When I was ten, this made no sense to me. How could you get farther behind if you're working faster and faster? Now, a few decades later, I know exactly what Mom was trying to say. There would always be something else to do, no matter how much you had done. Her message: Be happy with what you've completed and let the rest go.

That's why I'm toying with a fourth list: The *Don't-Do List*.

This list includes the stuff I think needs to be finished (and only by me) but no one will notice or care if it's done. Here's where the magic of lists works in my favor. I've discovered that if I write something on a list—*any* list—it removes it from my thoughts. The task is recorded somewhere and that's all that matters in my mind. If it really needs to be done, it will be taken care of someday, some way, and maybe not by me, so now I can let it go.

The first few things to get added to the New Year's Don't-Do List:

- Gather the paperwork for our tax lady;
- Clean out the junk drawer;
- Organize the Christmas gift bags by size;
- Scrub the shelves in the pantry;
- Delete old e-mails.

The New Year is a chance to start with a clean slate. It's a new beginning. A chance to reflect on the goals you didn't accomplish last year and an opportunity to put a plan in motion for future success. This year, my goal is to minimize the *to-do's*, enjoy the *dones* and increase the *want-to-do's*.

I wish us all a year filled with less to do and more time to do it.

Balancing the Scales

My *Deluxe Diet Scale* sits on my home office desk. I bought it a dozen or so years ago. It's one of many tools I've collected, all promising to help me reach my perfect weight. This ideal number isn't the same weight I enjoyed in my single days or even the weight I carried on my wedding day. No, I'm not that foolish. I know the difference between real and fantasy. My days of weighing less than my bowling score have long passed. I aim toward a sensible weight for my diminutive stature.

On the inside, I think God made me short for my weight, but that doesn't help my cause. So, like many women, I struggle with the number that lights up on my digital scale each morning. Yes, it's that same five pounds that I've tried to lose through four presidential administrations, only now it has doubled. It seems to be gaining momentum, fighting every step of the way to remain a part of me.

When I was twelve, I didn't think about how much I weighed or how my clothes fit. I never climbed on a scale unless it was at the doctor's office. The details that filled my mind as a curly-haired preteen were: Does Steve Newton, the handsomest guy in eighth grade, know I exist? How will I finish my next Girl Scout badge? What time does *The Partridge Family Show* start on TV and does David Cassidy have a girlfriend? Never a care about how many calories there are in a Strawberry Nirvana Jamba

Juice. Who thought about how much fat there is in movie theatre popcorn? Not me.

The lesson my mother wanted me to learn was that the girl I was mattered more than the girl I looked like. Her buzzwords were: *try, try again* and *always be truthful*. There weren't conversations about being overweight or how I looked. Short of combing my hair and making certain that my teeth were brushed, she never harped on these topics.

Sure, I recall Mom moving a yellow vinyl-covered chrome-legged kitchen chair in front of our black-and-white TV where she would do her leg lifts guided by Jack LaLanne. To me, her efforts were more in the spirit of exercise than weight loss. Fitness was the motto, not foxy.

But times changed and even though it's not what I learned at home, I have acquired a preoccupation with calories. Was there a time I didn't know my body mass index? I'm not sure. I think this transformation from happy-go-lucky schoolgirl to appearance-minded career woman happened slowly. It hit somewhere between young bride and seasoned mother.

I marvel at this plastic scale. It's divided evenly in ounces (and grams) and I realize that I haven't used it for its original purpose in a long time. I'm a bit ashamed to admit that in recent years, this measuring tool has been employed more often for weighing letters than for weighing spaghetti. As the price of postage expanded, so did my hips.

My doctor offers lots of convincing reasons why it's important to reach my goal weight. Things like a healthy heart and lower blood pressure top the list. But I think it's more than wanting to live to see my grandchildren that inspires me to skip the extra serving of guacamole and stay away from the office Krispy Kremes. My real motivator, in spite of Mom's insight, is the quest to look young. In this age of face-lifts and tummy tucks, who wants to be labeled fat and frumpy? Elastic-waist polyester pants and free-form blouses that aren't designed to be tucked in…no way. This is the generation of "good-looking, tight-fitting" jeans. I have a waistline and I want to use it.

My mind flips back to when I was that young Girl Scout, outfitted in my mint green uniform and dark green sash, dotted with badges. Alongside girls from my troop, I stood in front of the Market Basket grocery store, selling cookies. I didn't know about trans fats. Nutrition facts weren't printed on the side panels of the sandwich cookies we pedaled for fifty cents a box. Being together, having friends, and sharing a common goal was our priority—that and hoping that Randy Deveraux, the cutest boy in the fifth grade, would notice *one* of us.

I'll still use my scale to weigh occasional letters and care packages before I send them to my away-at-college son Jake. When I pull it out, though, now I'm aware of its intended purpose: an aid in reaching my ideal weight.

But a scale can never measure the person I am. Only I can assess that. I know that *ideal* exists only in my own expectations. This doesn't mean I'm giving up on watching my weight. I'm no quitter. Of course, I'll try, try again, no matter which way the scale tips. I think Mom would like that.

LOVE, ROMANCE, AND MARRIAGE

How My Garden Grows

Like many moms, I took time to garden with my kids, Shawn, Jake, and Seth. We planted sunflowers in early spring and watched them skyrocket past each young boy's head by the time summer arrived. I've tried daffodils, tulips, and sweet peas—all flowers guaranteed to grow easily for the novice gardener. I also dabbled in spearmint and basil. No luck. I have had great success with rosemary, but I think that's due to nature, not my nurture. My healthiest plant is silk.

I used to brag about my success in growing shamrocks. Then the neighborhood florist told me they were really weeds. That's when I gave up embracing horticulture with any passion. I've seen Ireland's forty shades of green and my thumb doesn't qualify for even the lightest hue.

The true gardener in our family is my husband Nick. He unwinds from the stresses of the workday by digging in the dirt, watering our trees, and pruning errant branches. It's therapeutic to him. Nick lives to grow things. Each March, underneath the warmth of spring sunshine, he charts out a strategy and anticipates a fruitful harvest from the great outdoors, also known as our backyard. He finds joy as he watches the miracle of the planted seed erupt through the soil and in weeks, become part of the bounty for our dinner table.

By the end of summer, he'll gather homegrown tomatoes, zucchini, bell peppers, and cucumbers, and proudly set them on the kitchen counter. We have the juiciest oranges, limes and lemons. He's innovative, too. His arboricultural efforts have created a half-lemon/half-lime Sprite tree.

With all of his success, one goal alludes my sweetheart—producing baskets full of avocados. Living in a warm climate, you'd think it wouldn't be a tough task. Sadly, my husband has yet to see enough fruit to make a medium-sized bowl of guacamole. Last year his harvest yielded four fist-sized avocados. We rejoiced as he gingerly carried them inside the house and scurried to place them in a brown bag so they would ripen quickly.

In the back of my mind, I wondered how much that quad of alligator pears had dinged the family budget. A full-grown tree needs at least 150 gallons of water per week in fall, summer, and spring. I'm guessing a price tag of about $27.50 each in water, fertilizer, and productivity.

Nick could have been tending my rose bushes.

My sons support their dad's efforts. Who doesn't love fresh guac? But they've learned to be guarded in their enthusiasm. When called to view the newest flowering or sprout, they approach with caution. Avocados are sensitive like their growers and don't like to be handled. Nick will excitedly point out the number of future avocados hanging from the tree. Poor Jake, in his haste to share in this father's excitement, barely tapped a pea-sized bud dangling from a branch, only to watch it—and my husband's face—fall to the ground. Nick picked up the ball and cradled it as though it were a sickly kitten in need of medical attention.

Nick's hopes for an improved output are high this season. Last week we made the trip to the home improvement store for seedlings, plants, and mulch. The longing in his blue eyes was clear and true as he placed the usual vegetable, herb, and spice selections in the cart. Hope springs eternal. "We're sure to see a return on that investment," he said.

That was when Nick spotted a clerk in a nook of the garden center and abandoned his cart to me. He cornered the elderly gentleman seeking the secret to robust avocado trees. Sincere head nodding and serious conversation were exchanged as Nick absorbed foolproof advice. I pretended not to notice. I worried that Nick's expectations would exceed results and by Labor Day he'd be disappointed once again. There was a handshake and by the time he lumbered back to the cart, he held a twenty-pound bag of nutrient-rich fertilizer. "This is what I've been missing," Nick said, heaving it into the cart. I wasn't convinced and started considering ways to attach mature avocados to tree branches in late August.

It was in that moment I realized my husband's tenacity. He won't give up. For him, spring is the season of new beginnings and second chances. The great outdoors renews itself and shows a fresh face. Nick will lovingly tend to his garden—digging, weeding, watering, and perhaps praying. His avocado trees will receive extra TLC and maybe by fall they'll produce enough to invite the neighbors over for a bowl of homemade tortilla soup, topped with grown-by-Nick avocado slices. If not, I can send the gang home with a fistful of shamrocks and a few sprigs of fresh rosemary.

After all, there's always next spring.

It's A Date

When I was in high school, dating was straightforward and spontaneous. All I needed was a good-looking guy to ask me out. Things didn't get much more complicated years later when I was dating my future husband. During our courtship and after we were first married, date night had few parameters and almost no planning. Our dates involved meeting at a predetermined time for dinner (cooked by someone other than me) and tickets to an event (movies, football game, a play).

The only thing necessary for the two of us to go out BK (before kids) was that we both were awake. Once our sons were born, everything changed. With the time it took to keep up with our threesome, not to mention the house and earning a living, the extravagance known as date night got relegated to the bottom of the list. We had more compelling things to do, like grocery shopping, helping with book reports, and making sure there was enough money in the checkbook to cover the house payment.

Nowadays, a quick trip to the Home Depot for the two of us to price out ceiling fans might qualify as a date. Who knew that spending time choosing wall sconces could be romantic?

When the boys were little, we were fortunate to have a willing granddad and two grandmoms living nearby. A simple phone call would secure a date night and, if we were really lucky, an occasional date weekend. While grandchildren and grandparents shared quality time, Nick and I would reminisce about how life was before three small people called us Mom and Dad.

The boys got bigger and the grandparents got older. It became apparent that if the two of us wanted to be alone together, other than when we're asleep, we'd have to come up with a new strategy. This strategy was intricate and required organizational skills normally reserved for air traffic controllers. Oh, and yes, the good will and the inherent need of fifteen-year-olds for spending cash.

That's when Nick and I developed an appreciation for our neighborhood teenage babysitters. We rotated among three and prayed that none of them got a boyfriend or found a job. That would signal the end to our scheduled independence. If Annie, Gretel, or Melissa had other plans for Friday night, we were sunk, along with those coveted tickets to the Smokey Robinson concert.

It's not that we didn't enjoy our quality time together cheering the kids on at soccer, baseball, basketball or football games. But face it, there's something to be said for the magic of sitting in a restaurant, alone with your husband, salad fork in hand. And, there's no sporting equipment of any kind zinging past your head.

Competition among other parents with small children was keen. It was imperative that we set ourselves apart from other *parents-in-need-of-a-babysitter.* We did everything we could to ensure that we were on the top of the babysitters' "yes" list when we called. Little things like an abundantly stocked refrigerator—sodas, yogurts, and lots of ice cream treats in the freezer—and a pantry filled with M&Ms, Oreos, and Cheetos go a long way to insuring a sitter for New Year's Eve. A plentiful supply of junk food combined with a generous hourly rate and a good tip guaranteed the Faddens a top spot in the babysitting world. About the time I thought I had the teen babysitter scene wired, though, a new development arose.

Our oldest son Shawn turned twelve. And then it seemed liked mere minutes before the other two caught up. Being perceptive, insightful parents, we could no longer ask teenagers to babysit our preteen son. Or at least that's what he told us.

That's when we began exploring co-op sleepover-babysitting. This approach relies on cultivating friendships with the moms and dads of our kids' friends. That and sharing a common goal—wanting a few minutes alone with your spouse. I'm a real fan of this method. It's a win-win if you do it right. Basically, parents take turns as the babysitter, and the kids love it. A typical scenario goes something like this: *If you let Jake stay at your house this weekend, then we'll have Chad spend the night for the weekend you have a wedding to attend.* Who can pass up that offer?

We've had to become resourceful when it comes to date night. It was easier when I was a teenager, but because of all Nick and I go through just to split a tub of popcorn and see a movie, we appreciate our time alone more. Maybe it takes some planning, but at least I don't have to worry if the boy will call me again or if he still thinks I'm cute. And I know where I can find him. When that boy isn't on a date with me, he's probably in the backyard playing catch with three people who call him Dad.

Chick Flicks

Chick flick (n) a movie that appeals to women more than men – Macquarie Dictionary Book of Slang

My husband Nick loves macho movies. Anything with John Wayne, Clint Eastwood, Chuck Norris, tanks, horses, or car chases will do. While I prefer to watch *An Affair to Remember* for the twentieth time, Nick would rather wheel around the TV dial to find a channel showing *The Godfather* or *Rocky*. The odds are in his favor, considering both films have numerous sequels. Which makes me wonder why there's no *When Harry Meets Sally Again* or *Pretty Woman II*?

Movie selection is a delicate area of negotiation in our marriage. Actually, it's a battle zone where differences in taste can find one of us unhappy at the box office. At upward of $8 a ticket, the cost of popcorn and Sno-Caps, not to mention securing a babysitter, going to the movies is an expensive proposition. It requires financial and emotional investment. That's why we need to choose wisely.

To his credit, Nick has suffered through many chick flicks. Over the years, he's learned to come prepared with a wad of tissues. He's taken a liking to rating each movie by the number of tissues I use during the matinee. If I've gone through ten or more, he dubs the film a real tearjerker. Since I cry at the drop of a sad McDonald's commercial,

I'm not so sure his tissue scale is an accurate assessment. I still well up every Christmas when Frosty melts. An especially touching phone ad can have me sobbing in seconds. This man who watches all the Halloween movies—without flinching—has a tough time sitting through love stories with his weepy wife.

So how do two adults cross this chasm of movie differences? In a marriage where we agree on everything from potty training to politics, could our varied tastes in cinema be a deal-breaker? Not in our case. We're a forward-thinking couple who puts their marriage first. That's why we've devised these strategies to insure marital movie bliss.

1) Take turns choosing movies to go see. (Unwritten rule 1a): If the film you pick is really bad, you forego your next movie-selecting opportunity.)

2) Take one for the marriage and tolerate a film that's not your favorite. I consider this strategy as falling under the "For better or for worse" part of my marriage vows.

3) My favorite solution: Mom's Night Out. (AKA: Dad's Escape from a Chick Flick.) The magic inherent in this strategy is simple. Instead of this wife dragging her beloved husband to a film he'll hate, I gather my girlfriends to enjoy a romantic comedy or a musical.

Why are girlfriends better company at these movies? Well for one thing, my friends don't mind if I cry. They're too busy crying themselves. A well-done chick flick lets you leave the theatre with a light-hearted *ahhhh* feeling, instead of a stomach-wrenching *aw*-ful feeling. So much the opposite of macho movies—no blood and guts, no one dies a violent death, and the girl always gets her man.

Guys don't get it. It's okay, though. They don't have to.

Nick and I appreciate our agreement. Instead of him suffering through movies he thinks are "a little slow," I put out the call for Moms' Night Out. Sometimes it's the soccer/football/baseball moms. Other days, my sisters make time for these adventures in cinematography.

These unselfish women have saved Nick (and their own husbands, too) from sitting through *Secrets of the Ya-Ya Sisterhood*, *Under the Tuscan Sun*, *The Book Club* and *Me Before You*. Nick is eternally grateful to my gal pals. I suspect their spouses are, too. These dads rise to the occasion and make certain that their brides are available for this valuable marriage-strengthening therapy. They know this is important to the success of their relationships. These are guys who recognize the significance of the call. Or maybe they're afraid of sitting through a showing of *Something's Gotta Give*.

Either way, this lady is committed to keeping her marriage happy, so I'll do what I have to do. And if that means planning regular chick flick movie dates, so be it. Of course, my steady date has first right of refusal. I'd never see a motion picture with the girls that Nick wants to see. Our movie dates now center on films we both want to see; making us happy, popcorn-eating, soda-drinking cinema patrons who respect each other's viewing preferences.

So come on Hollywood, do your part to preserve my relationship. Before you make *Rocky VII* or *Terminator V*, produce *Like Water For Chocolate II* and *Sabrina, the Sequel*. The future happiness of my marriage is depending on it.

The Lingo of Love

"What do you want for Valentine's Day?" my
husband asked earlier this month.

To the untrained ear, that might sound like a simple
plea for guidance. An innocent bystander would probably
say Nick was just asking how I wanted to celebrate this
year's February 14.

But husbands talk in a dialect all their own, and
wives spend years translating that jargon. As an expert in
Nick-speak, I knew this man of mine was really asking:
"Do you actually want me to pay $100 for roses that will
die in a week? And you don't want to go out to dinner and
fight the restaurant crowds, do you?"

Somewhere hidden in between the vows—*for better
or worse, for richer or poorer, in sickness and in health*—is
an unspoken agreement implying that to stay on the good
side of marital bliss, a bride must learn to listen like a wife.
In the early years of my marriage, I was a quick study. Like
most resilient women I discovered that I was equal to the
challenge. Mastery of the lingo didn't come overnight, but
after a bit of practice, I became an expert in this offshoot of
the English language I lovingly call *husband-speak*. Now
my practiced ear picks up the nuances necessary to
translate the words Nick says into the words Nick really
means.

The latest test of my translating talents was last
Thursday morning. Nick and his recently upgraded smart

phone were at the kitchen table, enjoying a cup of coffee together. Meanwhile, I was in our bedroom, getting ready for the day. Off in the distance, I heard a familiar voice call out: "My cell phone is on Casablanca time."

At first I couldn't tell if he was bragging or complaining. Then my mind switched from *what-should-I-wear-today* mode into *wife-figuring-out-husband-speak* mode. I realize that this innocent-sounding statement was a thinly disguised call for my help. Nick was really saying: "Help me fix this. Can you change my phone back to Pacific Standard Time?"

He was seeking assistance from me. Me, the woman who had a digital camera for a year before she opened the box. (I didn't trust my photos to a camera that didn't have a place to put a roll of 35mm film.) I no more knew how to change a setting from Casablanca time to California time than I know how to write a symphony or set up a Snapchat account.

For a moment I thought that he confused me with our sixteen-year-old tech-savvy son. Alas, no. He was enlisting me, his life partner, to come to his aid. After a half-hour of banter that included: "push the thingamajig," "scroll down to settings," and "how do I scroll down to settings?" this technologically-impaired couple conquered the cell phone together.

It's not so bad becoming a linguist when you love your husband. In fact, if you keep a positive attitude, you can make a game out of translating. It's a chance to solve a mystery. The way I see it, if I was an expert at pig Latin in fifth grade, I must have enough brain cells to understand my guy most of the time.

Cracking the code is key to keeping the lines of marital communication working smoothly. I think most women would agree. I know my friends do. And with all that we've learned about this special language over the years, we could probably teach a course for Berlitz.

Here's my contribution to that collective brain trust, a few common phrases to jot down in your own *Husband-Speak 101* primer.

Question: "Honey, what did we get Paul for his birthday?"

Translation: "I hope you remembered that it's my brother's birthday tomorrow and that you bought a gift and a card and it's all wrapped up and ready to go."

Question: "Claire, have you seen the remote?

Meaning: "Why are we watching the Hallmark Channel when there's a playoff game on ESPN?

Comment: "I have to take the car into the mechanic."

Request: "Can you follow me down to the repair shop, so I don't have to wait around for them to drive me home?"

Question: Did you buy any jalapeño-stuffed olives?

Plea: I can't find the jalapeño-stuffed olives.

Question: "What's for dinner?

Translation: "What's for dinner? (Occasionally husbands do say what they mean.)

Since I have a lot of in-the-marriage training, I was very careful how I answered Nick's Valentine's Day question. My reply was honest and direct: "Honey, you don't have to buy me anything. I know that you love me," I cheerfully said, kissing his cheek. "Don't go to any trouble."

I'm hoping he translated my words into: "You better not come home without flowers, chocolates, and a card. And if you think I'm cooking dinner, you must be out of your mind."

Lucky for me, Nick is fluent in *Claire-speak*.

Make Mine Diamonds

We were out to dinner with friends the other night when the topic of wedding anniversaries came up. Actually, in between appetizers and the main course, I brought it up. I knew Paul and Sue's fortieth was next month and I wondered how these two would mark the milestone occasion. They traded knowing glances. "We haven't decided yet," Paul volunteered.

Always the helpful soul, I piped up with my trademark suggestion: "You know that's a diamond anniversary!" My husband Nick rolled his eyes, frowned, and then added, "She says that about every anniversary."

I smiled at Nick. He'd know. I've chanted this rallying cry pretty much since the day we joined hands to cut our wedding cake. Whether it's the first or the fifty-first, I believe every wedding anniversary should be celebrated, acclaimed, and lauded. And, for my money, nothing says celebration like a pair of diamond earrings or a diamond anniversary ring. Successfully navigating the ups and downs of forty years of wedded bliss is certainly worth a diamond or two, so I put in a plug. Sue took a sip of her drink, smiled back at me, and the guys changed the subject to last night's baseball game.

Out of curiosity, the next day I looked online to find out what the anniversary experts had to say on the subject. I'm in favor of taking the guesswork out of shopping, but these guidelines (divided into traditional and modern suggestions) postpone the good stuff until many decades of being Mr. and Mrs. have passed. This sequence seems backward to me. Is this what the American National Retail Jewelry Association had in mind in 1937 when they first devised the list?

If Paul conformed to tradition, he would give Sue rubies—not diamonds—to commemorate their two score years of marriage. Rubies are nice, but why the forty-year delay? And if Paul follows those same traditional gift-giving gurus, Sue would spend the next twenty years anticipating diamonds.

It makes sense for young couples to exchange practical gifts when they're just starting out. I guess that's why suggestions like fruit, linens, and pottery show up for anniversaries one through ten. Some argue that working toward silver and gold, rubies and diamonds, are a great incentive to stay married.

I say phooey. Give your wife diamonds early and often. The monthly payments alone will keep you together for the next thirty, forty, or fifty years.

Guys, listen up. A wedding anniversary is the perfect time to go off script; or in this case, off list. My husband has done this a time or two. For our second anniversary, instead of the recommended cotton, he opted for boogie boards. For our eleventh, he bypassed steel and got me an espresso machine. Not exactly a sparkling tennis bracelet, but it's a start. He received a gas barbecue grill.

For our last anniversary, the "list" didn't offer any traditional gift recommendations. The modern suggestion touted furniture. Just what every girl wishes for; a new chifforobe. Nick wasn't thrilled, either. He was hoping for golf clubs. True to form, I proposed diamonds. Nick responded with granite (countertops). I'm not complaining. Granite is a sturdy substance; not as strong and shimmery as diamonds, though. Still it's much better than a coffee table.

Later this year, my husband and I are gearing up for a milestone anniversary of our own. In an few months we will mark what's traditionally known as the Pearl Jubilee. And believe it or not, the modern gift idea is diamonds. After all these years, I could legitimately finagle some ice out of my groom. But Nick had a better idea; a voyage to the land of his heritage—Ireland. It didn't take me long to swap the promise of diamonds for emeralds of another sort.

And since a trip to the Emerald Isle is way better than a single piece of jewelry, I've put my *Every Anniversary is a Diamond Anniversary* crusade on hold. Nick knows the truce is temporary. Once we return, I'll be back to lobbying for my cause with the same enthusiasm Herbert Hoover's campaign used when promising a chicken in every pot.

Well, at least that's my plan. Of course, I could be talked out of an ice-crusted bauble in exchange for a champagne toast, a foot massage and a warm, tender kiss from the same man who, year after year, continues to say "I do."

It's Got to be a Guy Thing

My husband Nick and I have lots in common. We share the same religion. Voted for the same man for president. Cheer on the same NFL team. We even parent three sons together. For sure, he's the one I want bringing me a bouquet of roses and a box of chocolates on February 14.

But over the years, I've noticed that our personalities collide—a lot. Nick likes westerns. I prefer comedies. My car radio is set to R&B, his to classic rock. I like cake. He'll take pie.

Nick was born in Newark and I'm from a little town near Pittsburgh. I used to wonder if that was the root of our differences. Then I thought, maybe it's because I'm the youngest of four and Nick is the seventh of nine. Or perhaps it's because I have brown eyes and his are blue.

But the realization of a simpler answer trumped my earlier theories—men and women are different. When I was playing with Barbies, Nick was setting up his Hot Wheels track. When he was being introduced to Barbasol, I was learning about mascara.

About three weeks ago, our contrasting preferences became even more apparent. I invited him to go shopping at the mall. I figured that our trip would take up most of Saturday afternoon and part of the evening. Nick was planning on a thirty-minute outing (travel time included).

Not only do Pinks and Blues differ when it comes to how long a shopping trip takes, we're oceans apart about what we want to shop for. Ogling the latest in barbecue accessories or scoping out bug spray in Home Depot is Nick's idea of the ultimate buying expedition.

For me, the mark of a successful mall visit is finding the perfect pair of shoes—no matter how long it takes. Before I became a wife, I thought that everyone loved shoe shopping. Nick has since taught me that if you circle Male instead of Female on credit applications, you probably don't consider footwear as a personal fashion statement.

About an hour later, from across the winter boots display, my husband sent a pained look my way. I was veering into the purse department. Of course there was a basketball (football, baseball, soccer, golf, hockey, curling, bowling) game on TV and I suspected that he'd rather be watching a six feet six dude take three-point-shots instead of discussing the merits of pebbled leather. Or giving his opinion about which looks better, the hobo bag or the tote? What he really wants to say is: "Don't you have a dozen purses in the closet already? Pick one of these and let's get home before the third quarter ends."

Men and women are on shaky ground when it comes to problem solving, too. Women understand that sometimes all you need is a listener who nods supportively and mutters "Hmmmm" at suitable intervals. Just because we pose the question, doesn't mean we're looking for the answer. Men, on the other hand, are programmed to fix things—here's the problem, here's the solution, end of story.

This is where my husband shows his royal blue streak. His problem-solution skills are right up there with some of the greatest minds of his gender: Einstein, FDR, Knute Rockne. But after this short discussion the other morning, Nick won't be so quick with the answers anymore:

"Boy, I don't like the way these pants look," I said, glaring at the mirror.

"They are a little tight," Nick observed. "How's your diet going?"

"Slowly. Why are you asking?"

"Because you said you didn't like the way your pants fit. You could always do what your friend did and try liposuction."

"I didn't say they didn't fit. I said I didn't like how they looked. I don't like this khaki color."

"Ohhhhh…" he sheepishly replied.

I'll leave you to imagine the rest of the conversation, but you can be sure that Nick will never again suggest liposuction to his bride. In his spare time, he's now practicing variations of: "Claire, you look great in whatever you wear."

It's true that I might be from Venus and sometimes Nick wishes he was on Mars, but after many years of marriage, we're proof that opposites attract. It may be a girl thing and it might be a guy thing.

But one thing's for sure—thanks to an odd-colored pair of capri pants, this Valentine's Day I'll be getting a larger bouquet of roses. And that box of chocolates I told you about earlier is certain to be a three-pounder.

A Wedding, A Parade, A Family Affair

Nick and I didn't disappoint anyone. That's why our wedding spawned a cast of thousands—well, maybe dozens—actually, eighteen. We tried to include as many members of his Irish-Catholic family and my Maronite Catholic one that we could.

I—the youngest of four—had a variety of nieces, nephews, and godchildren, all the right shapes and sizes to be ring bearers and flower girls. Nick, the seventh of nine, nearly had a baseball-team's worth of brothers and sisters to cast in various wedding roles.

We did our best to find roles for almost everyone. We even invented positions: junior bridesmaids, alternate best man (would assume best man duties should the first candidate become unable to do so) and auxiliary bridal-party members.

The day finally came, with aunts and uncles, cousins, and high school friends making the journey to show their support and maybe tack on a San Diego vacation. The organist began and my parade of bridesmaids, donning wide-brimmed garden hats crowned with white daisies, ambled down the aisle. Then I heard the starting chords of "Here Comes the Bride."

The rose petals that my flower girls, Frances and Melissa, dropped so precisely, guided my steps along the white satin runner. I smiled at neighbors and friends lining the pews. Could they detect the quivering baby's-breath laced through my flowing bouquet of yellow roses?

Then I saw Nick for the first time, standing tall and looking handsome. I was awash in the faces of the people I cared about most in the world. They surrounded us with smiles, encouragement, and most of all, love. As my brother George placed my hand in Nick's, I saw hope, compassion, and affection in his eyes for his baby sister.

Why did we engage an entourage to witness our vows? After all, a wedding day is twenty-four hours to focus on us. It's a moment frozen in time when we pledged undying love, devotion, and our willingness to share the Pepsodent. A short jaunt to the justice of the peace would have been as binding as this colossal formal event at our church.

Truth is, a wedding is much more than an agreement to share utility bills and the remote. Marriage is combining two families (parents, siblings, cousins, pets, and nosy neighbors) together for a lifetime. And we wanted our families there to witness our commitment. We wanted them to share in our joy and shower us with love and support.

As a young bride and groom, we got caught up in the hoopla of insignificant details like which filling to put in the cake; when will the bachelor party be; and who will host the many showers. This naïve bride hadn't realized that the miles of tulle and lace would quickly be traded in for towels and Tide.

When we were spending time on figuring out how many guests sit at a table, we should have been mastering cooking terms like defrost, sauté, and stir. We were both the products of parents who managed to raise responsible kids, several of them. We were trying to pull off a colossal party when we could have been learning more about the families we were marrying into.

The wedding was a success. In fact, guests still tell us it was the best one they ever went to—a warm August day at the Coronado Cays clubhouse, when everyone danced to Sister Sledge's "We are Family."

I smile at the memory of seeing three (non-bridal party) friends vacationing from New Jersey wearing rented tuxedos because they hadn't packed anything else to wear. There was the loving toast our best man Leo offered; the dollars being pinned on my dress to the tune of "Fooled Around and Fell in Love" and the way a line of bunny-hoppers stretched the length of the clubhouse. We survived the wedding frenzy and the tribulations of fielding a bridal party the size of a soccer team. After the bedlam ended, it boiled down to two families becoming one.

Nick had become part Yezbak just as surely as I had become a Fadden. His parents, Anna Marie and Tom, quickly became Mom and Dad to me. And my mom, Florence, was now Nick's mom, too.

A few years passed before the two of us morphed into three and then four and then five, happily shifting the grandchild score to double-digits. Life busied us with lots of new-family challenges and decisions that come with parenting three sons.

But every once in a while, my thoughts turn back to that summer day, when a young girl from Pennsylvania, with everyone in the world looking on, took the hand of a young guy from New Jersey and began a California family of their own.

SCHOOL DAYS

Everything I Needed to Know

I Learned from My Sons' Kindergarten Teacher

Shawn's first day of kindergarten turned out to be my first day, too. I just didn't know it yet.

On that memory-making morning, I was stationed near the back of the classroom, excited to witness the start of my first child's formal schooling. I watched as he hung his backpack on a hook, found his nametag, and joined the other children. Armed with both photo and video cameras, my husband, Nick and I captured and recorded this milestone moment.

We joined a cluster of other rookie parents, *oooh*ing and *aaah*ing about our young scholars. Looks of hope and wonder, coupled with an eagerness to parent outstanding students, outweighed our inexperience. Kindergarten teachers recognize this look. Unfazed, they tackle the challenge of teaching five- and six-year-olds much more than how to print their name, recite their address, or where to line up for class. As part of the package, these teachers also accept a little acknowledged, but equally important job—training kindergarten parents.

Luck smiled on me when it chose my trainer. At the tender age of four years and eleven months, Shawn was placed in Mrs. Clow's class. As September gradually slipped into June, she guided me from rookie kindergarten parent to experienced mother of a student.

My first lesson came about four weeks into the semester. It was Shawn's fifth birthday and I'd taken off from work to bring in a special treat—homemade sugar-cone cupcakes. I was up past midnight the night before creating miniature cakes inside cones that didn't want to be used as molds. They weren't sturdy and easily tipped over, splattering chocolate cake batter everywhere. I didn't care. I was committed to these rainbow-sprinkled confections even though they continued their wobbly act as I transported them to class. I'd also brought each child an unsharpened zoo-themed pencil. I knew my efforts wouldn't go unheralded by Shawn and his classmates. My ears could hear their gleeful thank-yous.

My son beamed from where he sat in the reading circle when he saw me come in carrying boxes and bags. Perched on his head was a purple construction paper crown with a large, glittery number five written on the front. He also wore the class *Birthday Necklace*. Mrs. Clow signaled for me to go to the picnic tables to get ready for the party to take place before recess.

I carefully stood a homemade sugar-cone cupcake on each of the *Happy Birthday* plates. Even Rachel Ray would be proud of my efforts. Minutes later, my thoughts of greatness were squashed as I surveyed thirteen partially-eaten cupcakes and seven that just had the sprinkles licked off. Not only had my cupcakes bombed, but I was starting to hand out stick-like objects to twenty-some kids under the age of six. Pencil-driven sword fights would have broken out on the playground had Mrs. Clow not intervened.

Being a wise and patient woman, she helped me gather the would-be swords from the children. Calmly she suggested that it might be better to pass them out when the students left class that day. Her pleasant demeanor left no clue as to whether she recognized my potential or if she wrote off all hope of me being a responsible kindergarten parent.

Under her gentle indoctrination during the next several months, I learned about the world that is kindergarten. When I lamented that Shawn (and I) had a hard time finding photos of twelve things that begin with the letter R, she advised: "Go to the index of any shopping catalog." Sure enough, everything from refrigerators to raingear was there, complete with a page number to find a picture.

Conveniently, right before my second son Jake's birthday (some four years later), she mentioned that most kids aren't too excited about sugar-cone cupcakes. "They really love ice cream sandwiches," she said with a wink, "and they come twenty-four to a box. Just stash them in the cafeteria freezer with a note saying which class they're for and you're home free."

Mrs. Clow persevered and by the time Shawn and Jake reached the upper grades, a solid educational foundation was formed. Their mom was prepared for their future schooling, too. About that time, Seth, my youngest, was ready for kindergarten, and I finally got the job I'd been hoping for: stay-at-home mom. I knew he'd get the same strong start in Mrs. Clow's class that benefited his brothers. And what was even better, now I could devote more time to being a classroom volunteer.

I eagerly took on the task of room mother and looked forward to helping train new kindergarten parents. It was easy to spot them. Their faces were aglow with that same unknowing look I had eight years earlier. That, and on party day, they'd be toting a full sheet of birthday cake and nothing to cut it with.

Project Help

We watched as Seth attached the last piece of a strawberry splash fruit chew to his shoestring licorice and marshmallow replica of a DNA molecule. My husband Nick and I smiled at the finished product.

Three weeks earlier, Ms. Scott, Seth's high school biology teacher, challenged her class to be creative with this major homework assignment. "Think of new ways to display the double-helix structure of human DNA," she suggested. "Have some fun with it."

"I want my model to be entirely edible," Seth declared that night, excited about doing something out of the ordinary. So, some eight packages of fruit-flavored snacks, a few marshmallows and a bag of red licorice later, I witnessed the multi-night construction come to a close.

As my youngest child took pride in his efforts, I mentally patted myself on the back. I had come a long way as a recovering *help-my-child-with-every-school-project* mother. Other than driving him to the store to purchase supplies, Seth had done this assignment on his own. I took more satisfaction in that fact than the *A* he proudly displayed days later.

My desire to help too much with homework started innocently enough. When Shawn, my oldest, was in kindergarten, he asked for something to take to school that started with the letter A. Casually, he mentioned that he'd get extra credit if no other student brought the same thing.

The quest was on. Over the next few weeks, Shawn shared an abacus, bongos, a cloak and a deerstalker hat (think Sherlock Holmes) with his five-year-old classmates. By the time the kindergarteners had reached K, his backpack was laden with a kettle, a kazoo, a kaleidoscope and a kimono, each worth one extra credit point.

I worked on curtailing my overpowering offers-to-assist by the time Jake, my middle son, hit fifth-grade. For Colonial Days, he needed to produce something that portrayed life in the 1700s. After reviewing the options—including churning butter and making candles—we agreed on sewing a sampler. When I drove Jake to school on Colonial Day morning, I was very proud of our hoop-framed, cross-stitched piece of muslin that read: *Home Is Where the Heart Is.*

A convertible pulled up behind us and I wondered why the driver had the top down on this cold, rain-threatening day. Then I saw him and his fifth-grader lift a five-foot wooden pillory from the back seat. I wasn't the only parent who needed to lighten up about their child's school project.

I hoped that I'd found a nice balance between helping and observing by the time Seth reached middle school, but I was wrong. When the *My Life* health project came around, I was lured back into my old ways. Using words, photos, and illustrations, Seth needed to design a four-sided packaging label that showed who he was on the inside and then attach the label to the outside panels of a cereal box. Even though I thought the concept was clever, I was frustrated by my lack of artistic talent. How could Seth's cereal box design compete with students of creative parents?

While at work that week, I lamented this unfair assignment to my artistically gifted friend, Susan. "I can't draw a stick man, much less illustrate a cereal box."

"It's Seth's project, right?" Susan reminded.

"Well, yes, but every parent is *helping* their child," I said, remembering the life-size punishment device that garnered an A+ for both student and parent. "Those kids with parents who can draw will get the As," I said, convinced of the inequality.

That night Seth was surrounded by photos, drawings, markers, paper, glue and scissors splayed across the kitchen table. He'd asked me earlier to find an empty cereal carton and now he was busy writing.

I peeked over his shoulder to read his education and career goals. I scanned the section where he'd penned his five strongest character traits. Sandwiched between *loving* and *funny*, were *reliable, trustworthy,* and *honest.* Realizing that he had this under control, I reluctantly retreated to the den, occasionally calling out to see if he needed my help. He responded each time: "No, thanks." A few weeks later, he came home from school with an evaluation sheet taped to his "Seth's Life" cereal box. He earned an A++ and a "Super Project" comment from his teacher.

So years later, I watch as my son gingerly transfers his scientific work-of-digestible-art from the kitchen table into a cardboard tray so he can take it to class the next day. In spite of living with a mom who flies the *Let-me-help-you* flag every chance she gets, Seth stood on his own effort. Like his older brothers, Shawn and Jake, he wanted to fly his own flag, and on this day, it was in the shape of a DNA molecule.

What better way to show his dad and me his true character—all that cool stuff he so eloquently wrote about years before and glued to the outside of a cereal box.

The Most Wonderful Time of the Year

It's a little-known fact that my favorite TV commercial sells staples and sticky notes. Even my husband Nick would be surprised. He thinks that I'm partial to ads using the slogan: "A Diamond Is Forever." And I don't want to change his opinion. But just between you and me, my vote for best TV commercial goes to a purveyor of printer cartridges, file folders, and mailing labels. I'm quite the fan of a certain office supply megastore's ad campaign and it doesn't have anything to do with their glamorous wares, although I do like a nice pen.

Nevertheless, I tip my hat to the marketing mavens and mavericks who cleverly juxtaposed back-to-school shopping to the tune of "It's the Most Wonderful Time of the Year." During thirty quick seconds, this TV mini-movie acknowledges what parents of school-age kids secretly feel; Christmas doesn't come in December, it shows up in August or September. I've been comforted by this bit of retail genius through several school-shopping seasons and no matter how many times I've watched it, the commercial still makes me smile.

Andy Williams' voice croons happily while Dad skips, pirouettes, and glides down the store's aisles, cascading pencils into his shopping cart. Two sad-faced children reluctantly trail behind. This advertisement appeals to those of us who are glad to see our youthful seekers of knowledge return to education's hallowed halls. With a wink and a smile, we moms and dads covertly pump our fists into the air, or exchange high-fives as the first day of school approaches.

After the relaxed schedules of summer, we're relieved to be back in our school routine. Bedtime is reinstated and mornings find our young learners eating their cereal by 7:30. Students are out of the house (and in class) most days from eight to three. Yes, I treasure the first day of school almost as much as singing "Jingle Bells" and sipping eggnog. It is the most wonderful time of the year.

But, much like the holidays, I find that the actual preparation isn't nearly as much fun. Mere weeks after June's last day of class, my mailbox is bombarded with back-to-school circulars. I hold off on these door-buster sales, after learning the hard way not to guess how many glue sticks, color pencils and big pink erasers that year's teacher will require. I patiently wait for a "suggested list of school supplies" that finds its way into my hands every September.

Until my three sons started their formal education, I was oblivious to this annual shopping frenzy. As toddlers, Shawn, Jake, and Seth watched Sesame Street and learned to recognize the Letter and Number of the Day. Time passed and before long, they were ready to tackle a more demanding curriculum. At four-year intervals, shortly after turning three, each of them ventured into preschool. For a few hours, three days a week, they learned, courtesy of Miss Diane, Miss Sheila, and Miss Cathy, how to share, play well with others and line up for recess.

The preschool supply list was pretty short: the newest cartoon character lunch box, lace-up sneakers, and a fresh box of crayons. As the number of classroom hours increased, though, so did the educational necessities. Alongside spelling, social studies, and math came items like stretchy book covers, protractors, multi-themed binders and insulated lunch bags. Predictably, elementary school turned into middle school. The coursework became more complex and sophisticated. So did my boys. In addition to all the regular stuff, they now required essentials like hiker-style backpacks, graphing calculators, mechanical pencils, and laptops.

I discovered that hidden in between the shopping negotiations—how many pocket folders to buy and how much to spend for a pair of jeans—lies a parent's real reward for stocking desks, lunchboxes, and closets. We secure a front row seat to watching the future open up for our children. Pencil by pencil, we witness their growing excitement for learning and we encourage their dreams. Whether it's reciting the alphabet, earning an A+ on their science project, or making the team, we get to share their pride of personal achievements.

The semesters keep clicking by. In a few short years, Seth, my youngest, will trade in his textbooks, backpack, and supply list for a diploma, a resume, and a career. And I'll relinquish the task of comparing prices for index cards, pencil pouches, and combination locks. Even though my days as official school-supply buyer are coming to a close, I'll keep a place in my heart for a certain holiday commercial. I hope to watch it for years to come.

And while I'm humming along, maybe I'll give into the urge and buy some yellow highlighters in celebration of this most wonderful time of the year.

The Last Field Trip

Each of my sons has a baby book. Yes, my oldest son Shawn's book is the thickest, but he's been around the longest. The pages of Jake's and Seth's are full of photos, souvenirs, and mementos, too.

Even I have one. It's about a half-inch thick and there's not a lot in it. Being the fourth of four, Mom didn't have a ton of time to keep it up-to-date. Nick, my husband and seventh of nine, lost out on the baby book bandwagon altogether.

For eager moms and dads who don't want to miss a single one, baby books are a great way to keep track all the first times: the first tooth, the first step, the first haircut, the first success in the potty.

There are calendars that help with this task, too. I liked this easy method so I hung one on the wall above the changing table for all of my sons. Complete with colorful stickers that said: *discovers toes, creeps, holds spoon, plays peek-a-boo,* I knew I wouldn't miss a single, first-time event.

I even bought Seth a *Second Year Sticker Calendar.* I like to think I was more organized by then, but the truth is: with three kids, the baby books got pulled out less and less. My interaction with *sticker calendar* though, was predestined right along with every diaper change. It was a fast way to note when Seth gave his first "high-five"

(November 14), said "bye Daddy" (March 27), or turned pages in a book we were reading (May 1).

What I wonder, though is why there are no handy books and calendars to remind parents to record the lasts. No stickers that say "last time he…" Pretty much, moms and dads are on their own to develop a sixth sense, a detector of sorts, to recognize these moments.

All the things I thought would go on forever, vanish a little every day. The last crawl turns into the first step, the last day of third grade morphs into the first day of fourth grade. Endless stuff like reminding Seth to tie his shoes, packing crunchy peanut butter and jelly sandwiches for Shawn's lunch, or watching Jake pitch have already been replaced with the next first.

Being aware of the firsts somehow raised my awareness of the lasts, though. And when Seth came home with a permission slip for a field trip a few months ago, I knew one was on the way. I knew this might be the last time I could tag along with his class. I also knew I'd have to act fast to secure my spot on the chaperone squad.

Before he knew what hit him, Seth had my signed permission slip in hand and I was on my way to the Spanish class field trip to Old Town. This trip with a busload of eighth graders would be the final bead in my string of field-trip-mom outings. The days of supervising preschoolers at the bakery, second graders at the zoo, and sixth graders at SeaWorld were coming to an end. The good news was that I knew it. I could enjoy this last and not let it get lost in the day-to-day activities of parenting.

That's what made the last field trip so special. I knew what it was and took the time to savor it. I don't recall when Nick and I crept into Seth's room for the last time to retrieve a tooth tucked under his pillow. I don't know when he last believed in the Easter Bunny or the last time he asked for my help with his math homework. I was too busy being a mom to realize that these moments don't go on forever. But somehow, on this one rainy Friday morning, I was a mom-in-the-know, totally present for my last field-trip mom duty.

I know there's more firsts to come with Seth: his first date, his first driving lesson, his first time breaking curfew. My antenna is always up for the firsts. This is standard equipment in every mother, sort of like airbags in new cars.

Luckily for me, over the years I've managed to hone my "*lasts detector*." Even when mine is turned all the way up, though, I still miss a lot. But maybe, since Seth is my last, my detector operates on a higher frequency. Or at least, more frequently. I certainly hope so. That way this field trip won't be my final chance to spot those inescapable lasts. They're guaranteed to keep coming and at no extra charge, whether I notice them or not.

What's In Your Lunch Bag?

Of all the duties that come with being a mother of three, the one I dislike the most is packing school lunches. I've tried to avoid the entire "lunch-packing" fiasco by encouraging the boys to buy lunch in the school cafeteria. No dice. "It takes too long to get through the line," they moan. My kids want to spend their time on the playground instead of waiting for their food. They don't get this from me; give me food prepared by someone else over playing basketball anytime.

Oddly enough, there's more to packing a third-grader's lunch than you realize. The uninitiated mom thinks all that's involved is throwing a few things in a brown paper sack. *Voilá!* You're done.

Not so. Lunch packing in the 21st century is a high-stress assignment. It's right up there with deciding which cell phone company offers the best deal. Support groups are forming as we speak.

You can't send your child off to school with a nutritious lunch made up from what you have around the kitchen and expect it to be eaten. The days of pouring chicken noodle soup in a thermos and wrapping a bologna sandwich in waxed paper like my mother did are long gone.

Today's top-notch lunch-preparer has her finger on the pulse of lunch food trends, an assortment of kid-sanctioned, lunch-box-friendly coupons and a keen sense to buy goodies when they're on sale.

Not only that, but the designated lunch-packer determines the correct number of items that comprise a marketable school lunch. If you put in more than five, something gets thrown away. Less than five and you'll hear how starved your son was during geography.

I've broken down a prototype school lunch into categories: a main course (sandwich/chicken fingers/pizza slice); a snack item (crackers/pretzels/potato chips); a beverage (juice box/bag); a piece of fruit (apple slices/grapes/banana); and a sweet treat (cookies/scooter pie/pudding). Along with a napkin, items are lovingly placed in lunch box (kindergarten to third grade) or brown bag (fourth grade on).

Through astute detective work (asking why a melted Ding Dong is lining the bottom of a backpack), I've learned what gets eaten, what gets traded, and what probably lands in the school trash can.

Any kind of Lunchable - eaten.

Carrot sticks - traded.

Bruised PB and J sandwich (jelly leaked through the bread) - tossed.

Anything broken, melted or banged up in transit - returned home *(in case little brother wants it)*.

My sons, Shawn, Jake, and Seth, coach me about the format (cool/not cool) they prefer their lunch items to be supplied. Here's what I've learned so far:

Cool: Store-bought individual bags of Doritos.

Uncool: Snack-sized zipper bag filled with packaged-by-mom Doritos.

Cool: Anything left over from Taco Bell, Pizza Hut, KFC.

Uncool: Leftovers mom cooked.

Cool: A napkin.

Uncool: Same napkin with a handwritten love note.

Cool: Chocolate pudding cup.

Uncool: Forgetting to pack a spoon to eat the pudding cup with.

I strive to provide my sons healthy, nutritious food for their midday meal and, at the same time, keep them in a power position when the lunch bell trading begins. Reputations are at stake. My kids need to be ready to make deals. They're on the frontlines bargaining, exchanging, and swapping. So I keep on top of the volatile lunch food market. What's hot and what's not. What are trendy fifth graders eating this week?

You might think this is easy—to know what to pack and what not to pack. But you'd be wrong. There is no crystal ball; no *E! Entertainment* TV coverage; no financial advisers or websites where this information is posted. *The Wall Street Journal* doesn't offer *This Week in Lunch Box Futures*.

There's only one way to research this thing. Go to the source—the kids. They are keenly aware of the commercial value of their lunch bag contents. Garfield fruit snacks don't bring in what they did two years ago. Two Oreos might get you a Chips Ahoy and a half-eaten box of raisins. Individual-size Pringles and a taco Lunchable can put your child in a strong position to trade for pizza and a nutty bar.

That's why it's up to me—mother, nutritionist, cook, shopper, healthcare provider, personal trainer—to be a savvy shopper and fill those lunch boxes and bags with what the customer wants.

I'm comforted to know my sons—armed with Fruit Roll-ups—can barter for someone's chicken nuggets. And as they wolf down their lunches and head out to recess, maybe they'll eat something I packed, too.

1000 Things to Teach Them Before They Graduate

Seth, the youngest of my trio of sons, graduates from high school this month. Mixed in with the pride of his accomplishments comes the reality that I'm being demoted. The title that I've coveted for so many years—through measles and bowl haircuts, Little League and Halloween carnivals—will change.

For the third time in my mommy-hood career, I'll graciously accept the reclassification from Mom the Manager to Mom the Consultant. Yes, I've been through this before. First with Shawn, and then four years later with Jake. I know the routine. I'm familiar with the drill, but that doesn't make accepting the bittersweet reassignment any easier.

I know Seth still needs me, but not in many of the same ways that I've grown accustomed to. I'll expect phone calls like the one I got from Shawn when he didn't know how to fix his jammed garbage disposal. Or the e-mail from Jake asking for help on writing his resume before he interviewed for an internship. Kids always need their mother and father, but now I'm on a "need-to-know" basis.

And there's a lot I don't need to know.

In a couple months Seth will start college, enthusiastic to take on his next adventure while I wait in the background and wonder if I've done all I can to prepare him. My heart sees him as a five-year-old boy curled on our couch watching *Homeward Bound* for the umpteenth time and crying inconsolably as Shadow, a golden retriever, falls into an abandoned railyard shaft. Wasn't it just last week he asked why chocolate chips are brown? That same inquisitive kid now barrels out the front door—football playbook and Economics text in one hand and car keys in the other—ready to start his future.

No parent can completely prepare their child for every eventuality—heartbreak, unfair professors, mean bosses, flu-like symptoms, cold lattes, broken appliances, late paychecks, flat tires. But still we try. I look back on these eighteen years and hope my nurturing, guidance and love has equipped him to meet life's challenges.

Seth's world is changing and so is mine. And it's during transitions like this that we grown-ups try to make sense of things. We corral our own goals. Check off items from our *Things to Do Before I'm 30 (40, 50)* list. Jot down some new ones.

My husband Nick and I bought a copy of *1000 Places To See Before You Die*. So far, we've only flipped through the pages, but it won't be long until we actually have time to visit some.

I'm excited to start whittling down my travel to-dos, but blissful tourist thoughts are repeatedly interrupted by another list formulating in my mind: *1000 Things I Hope I Taught Seth Before Graduation*. This roster is a mishmash of sticky notes, random thoughts, and verbal cautions that trail behind him as he walks out the door. Important things like *don't wash your orange baseball shirt with your underwear; check the date on the milk carton before you make a bowl of cereal; don't get into a car with an unsafe driver*.

I'm sure there are more than a thousand things I've taught, either by example or lesson, to Shawn, Jake, and Seth. But since I am limited to about 800 words here, I'll share (in no particular order) the top few I hope sunk in.

When you can spare a moment, feel free to add the other 989.

1) Trust your instincts. They will lead you on the right path.

2) Common courtesy counts. *Please, Thank You, I'm Sorry, Pardon Me* are not on the endangered word list, so use them freely. Open doors for women and your elders. Pull the chair out for your date. Turn off your cell phone in public.

3) Stay grounded. You'll always have a home and two people who never tire of hearing about your victories, defeats, goals, and challenges.

4) You won't know unless you try. (I borrowed this one from my mother, Florence; to which she'd add, *try, try and try again.*)

5) Choose quality time over quantity stuff.

6) Break big projects into small pieces. Don't wait until the night before that twenty-five-page term paper is due to write it.

7) Little things count. Let that car merge in front of you. Pick up someone else's trash. Put the seat down. Recycle. Smile.

8) You love your family, but you choose your friends; so choose carefully.

9) Never compromise your health. It's your most valuable asset.

10) Pray. Pray some more.

11) Call your mother.

Mostly, I hope Seth knows how much his dad and I love, trust, and admire him. Right before our eyes, in what feels like mere moments, he transformed from a helpless infant to an inquisitive toddler to a typical teen.

Now he stands on the edge of manhood, a confident, responsible, capable adult. And if I do say so myself, Seth, you've done quite a terrific job.

Claire Yezbak Fadden

CELEBRATIONS

Birthdays on the Bubble

It was not until I saw my husband Nick standing ankle-deep in a wading pool of homemade bubbles that I realized I'd made a mistake. My son Jake, the birthday boy, and several of his eight-year-old pals wouldn't have agreed. They were running amok, bubble wands, hoops, and blower guns in hand, puffing, popping, and shooting bubble ammo at each other. They stopped occasionally at this plastic oasis to refuel their bubble-making implements. With garden hose in hand, a barefoot Nick was working hard to keep the supply plentiful. Occasionally he shot a grimace my way.

Our backyard, sloshed in homespun bubble sauce, had turned into a slip-and-slide soapy mess. I surveyed the good clean fun springing up around me and made a mental note: *Do not repeat when younger son Seth turns eight.*

In the months leading up to Jake's Bubble Blowout, he'd attended a circus party complete with clowns, pony rides, and a trampoline. And for some nutty reason, I felt compelled to match those festivities. I didn't want him embarrassed at soccer practice the following weekend. "Just cake and ice cream, huh, Fadden. Don't your parents love you?"

Trying to find balance between foolhardy and prudent, this easy, inexpensive, and fun way to spend a couple of hours lathered up inside my head. It never crossed this young mother's mind that gallons of bubbles and twelve third-graders mix about as well as a white tuxedo and a spaghetti dinner. I suppose that if you're crazy enough to combine the two, you deserve what you get.

My heart was in the right place, even if my mind had taken a brief vacation. Birthday parties are the social event of the preschool-elementary school set. Every mom wants her child's to be the best. The build-up starts weeks (and sometimes months) before. This year was no different. I ran lots of themes past Jake: cowboys, racecars, pirates. Nothing produced two thumbs-up from my middle child.

From our lengthy conversation I garnered that he wanted a party that:

1) was different (Jake ruled out having a magician. Anthony already had one. And Chad's mom was planning his roller-skating party for next month.);

2) had activities a bunch of eight- and-nine-year-old boys would want to do;

3) wasn't lame and boring (Jake's words, not mine) and;

4) was affordable enough not to compromise his college savings account (Okay. That one's mine.)

I remember the birthday parties my mother had for me. There wasn't one every year and the ones I did have were little more than cupcakes and fruit punch for the neighborhood kids. Nowadays, the bar is raised so high you'd think there was the *Country's Best Kid's Birthday Parties* show on the Disney Channel and we were vying for a slot.

Mind you, by this stage in my mommy-hood career, I wasn't a party-planning rookie. I'd successfully thrown several, including a dinosaur party, complete with tots—in parade formation—toting their favorite stuffed animal/dinosaur to the tune of "Baby Elephant Walk." I earned a gold star for inviting a Winnie the Pooh walk-around character to help play pin-the-tail on Tigger. Other winners: Bowling Bash, Teeing Off at Miniature Golf and Let's Go to the Movies.

But I've also masterminded a few catastrophes, the worst being my oldest son Shawn's October costume party. With equal measures of enthusiasm and naïveté, I invited all the boys in his kindergarten class *and* his entire soccer team—totaling some twenty-five masqueraders. Luckily, my mother-in-law Anna Marie (a seasoned mom and grandmom) was on hand to prevent me from total meltdown. She took it all in stride, slicing pizza, scooping ice cream, and controlling the long lines for apple bobbing.

I recall her gentle smile afterward as she counseled me. *"It's okay, honey. The kids had fun and you learned what not to do next time."* I thought I had learned my lesson until I saw Nick covered in soapsuds. In my excitement to throw a party that would be talked about for days, I threw one that might keep my husband from talking to me for weeks.

Many birthday parties have passed since my bubble fiasco. As routinely as the changing seasons, they've come and gone, incorporating the usual stuff: cake, candles, balloons, presents. But now there's one small modification: Nick has veto power of any theme *before* the invitations are sent out. It's purely a precautionary measure.

If for some reason I take leave of my senses and start planning another soapsuds soiree, he'll be the one to burst my bubble.

Birthdays from One to Ninety-Two

Anyone who has ever received a birthday card from me opens it carefully. They might even hold it over a trash can.

Why? They know I've stashed confetti inside, and they want to keep the mess to a minimum. I sneak a rainbow of glittery metallic chips between the folds of the card; my way of enjoying the party before it's even started. I love birthdays and when the confetti cascades out, along with my good wishes, my theory is once again affirmed.

And what theory is that, you ask? I believe that the joys and good feelings of a birthday are not limited to the person born on that date. They radiate to the rest of us sharing in the delight. Here's my proof:

1) We throw parties, rent air-jump bouncy houses, and fill piñatas in celebration of babies who can't even say "make a wish."

2) We plan birthdays for our elders who probably stopped counting their age about the time gas was under a buck.

I think this is a good thing. This is our way of saying *we treasure you*, whether you know it or not. We love you and care about you when you're young and sticking your hand in the icing; and we still love you long after you've stopped counting how many presents are stacked on the table.

I don't remember my first birthday, but I know I had one. I have a picture to prove it. A curly-topped toddler, sitting with her dad, mesmerized by a homemade three-layer cake. It sports one big candle and I can't tell if I blew it out yet or if I had to ask for help. This baby girl had no idea it was her birthday. A big cake, presents, aunts and uncles making a fuss over her were all proof that she was loved, long before she could ask for the newest Barbie dollhouse. It was important to my mom, my dad, my brothers, and my sister to celebrate the anniversary of the day I was born. So, there was a party. It didn't matter if I knew why.

My mother's ninety-second birthday would have been this month.

When she passed away two years ago, the party planning ended. That makes me more grateful for the memories of her past birthday celebrations, like her sixty-fifth, when our family scripted a version of *This Is Your Life* and her sisters flew to San Diego from Pennsylvania and West Virginia to surprise her. There was standing-room-only for her eightieth birthday. Family and friends trekked from all over the country for a summertime feast. My backyard was overflowing with well-wishers sharing a common purpose—their affection for a special woman.

The most recent memory is of her ninetieth birthday. It was the last party. And being true to her merrymaking spirit, she made it. Even though she was nearing the end of her battle with Alzheimer's disease, Mom wouldn't let her family and friends miss out on a good time. Balloons, flowers, and a sea of smiling faces, all poised to celebrate her nine decades of good living. The bewildered look on Mom's face revealed that she didn't know what the hullabaloo was all about. But that didn't matter. She was surrounded by love. Her children, grandchildren, and great-grandchildren were providing the excited chatter, laughter, and revelry. Just like that party held decades ago for an unsuspecting one-year-old, this celebration was for those who held a special love for the birthday girl.

This month, I will be planning birthday parties for Jake and Seth. Even if I combine the number of candles I'll put on their cakes, the total falls somewhere on the low end of the one-to-ninety-two range. All the usual things will happen. They'll get presents and choose what they want for their birthday dinner. They'll enjoy the hubbub and frenzy instigated by their parents, thinking that all this fuss is just for them. That's because they haven't embraced my theory. Yet. They still consider that their birthdays are just for them. They don't know that the pleasure is cherished and appreciated by the guests as much as the guest of honor.

Someday, though, they'll realize that life's enduring gifts are the ones you receive when it's not your birthday. They're the ones you give. And those presents are the ones you remember most, no matter if the birthday girl is one or ninety-two.

Merry Birthday. Happy Christmas.

This is my salute to Sagittarians and Capricorns—
my sisters and brothers all over the county who, like me,
have a birthday bordering the holidays. Each of us who has
known the disappointment, heartbreak, and misfortune that
comes with being born too close to Christmas. Through no
fault of our own (and because of the poor planning of our
parents), we were born on the fringes of the busiest, most
expensive holiday of the year.

We're forced to compete against giant evergreens,
cookie parties, and men in red suits, armed with nothing but
a candle, a party popper, and a handful of confetti. It's no
wonder December birthdays are often overlooked.

I like to think of us as an elite group—strong and
proud—celebrating our birthdays interspersed among office
Christmas parties, strolling carolers and the Nutcracker
ballet.

My birthday, for example, is December 15 (the last
day to mail packages at the post office for guaranteed
delivery before Christmas). It's not the easiest time of the
year to have a birthday. Most people wouldn't choose to be
born around Christmas. In fact, I feel so strongly about it
that when we were first married, I wouldn't let my husband
near me from March through mid-April. That's why none
of my three children have a birthday anywhere near the
holidays.

The closest one is Shawn's, whose birthday is in October. Halloween costumes on display, autumn leaves turning vivid oranges and browns, and pumpkin patches sprouting up. Very few sightings of candy canes, reindeer, or mistletoe.

Since Nick and my sons are all regular birthday people (born in March, July, and October) they really didn't understand a few necessary rules in the care and maintenance of my birthday celebration. Over the years, thanks to my patience and tutelage, they have learned a few ways to keep the happy in my birthday.

Don't give me ONE big present. I would much rather have TWO smaller ones—one wrapped in birthday paper and the other wrapped in paper featuring snowmen. If my birthday was June 15, Nick wouldn't even think about giving me one big present and then saying on December 25: "Remember in June, that robe we gave you for your birthday...?"

I want a regular birthday cake (yellow roses, a clown, some balloons). Nothing on the cake should remotely be associated with the holidays (no candy canes, snowflakes or holly). The cake shouldn't resemble the North Pole. Stay away from red and green icing.

Please don't wrap my birthday present in Christmas wrap (a major no-no). And don't try to disguise the paper by turning it inside out. I'm on to that trick.

For years, before my sons figured it out, I didn't put up the Christmas tree until after my birthday. That tradition has faded. We're usually trampling through tree farms on Thanksgiving weekend. Compromise: no presents placed under the tree until after birthday presents have been opened.

I don't want to go to the office Christmas party on my birthday. Fortunately, Nick can manage to schedule his company's holiday get-together on a different day. Thank you, honey.

Just like everyone else, we Holiday Babies want the date we were born on to be a celebration in our honor. Is blowing out the candles and making our wish without listening to "Santa Claus is Coming to Town" blaring in the background too much to ask?

For me, it's not all about getting a cavalcade of gifts. It's about being remembered on my special day. A card, a phone call, or an e-greeting saying "I'm thinking of you today" is perfect. (Don't confirm that fact with Nick, though. Over the years he's gotten the impression that I want one gift for every year of my age. Recently he's taken to just ordering dozens of roses to cover his bases.)

So, fellow Sagittarians and Capricorns, this December I'm wishing you a very happy birthday filled with balloons, gifts, and even an off-key rendition of the Beatles classic, "You Say It's Your Birthday."

Maybe in our next lives things will change and we'll be the ones born in April instead of December. Not only is April a good seven months before the Christmas shopping season starts, but those lucky enough to be born that month get diamonds instead of blue topaz as their birthstone.

Writing on Eggshells

I've managed to dye my fingers a new shade of purple, a color not found in any box of crayons. It falls somewhere between eggplant and magenta. As I stare at my hands, I wonder if the stain will fade before next weekend when I'm going to my cousin's wedding. I guess I can always wear gloves.

Just moments ago, I was surrounded by a quartet of eager egg-colorers happily decorating oval orbs in a rainbow of hues. Now the decorators are gone and I'm left alone, near a plastic bowl holding four dozen hard-boiled eggs. I survey the damage, once known as the surface of my kitchen table. I thought I'd learned my lesson from last year's Easter egg-coloring fiasco. That's why I painstakingly blanketed the table with layers of yesterday's newspaper, but somehow a pinkish-green dye managed to find the one unprotected triangle. The oak grain now possesses a colorful, confetti-like stain. I decide that this botched job is not a commentary on my table-covering abilities; it's directly related to the five people vying for space around six coloring cups.

Mess or not, the Coloring of the Easter Eggs is a key element in our family's springtime traditions that include new clothes, egg hunts, and baskets full of chocolate bunnies. It's these customs that I count on year after year to replenish my little-girl-at-heart spirit and keep me on track as mother. As a child, Easter meant a frilly bonnet, new patent leather shoes and the promise of a basket to be filled and hidden by the Bunny. My family has their own ideas about how to welcome spring.

Twenty minutes earlier, I watched my sons participate in their own Easter memories. They balanced their eggs on the rim of a flimsy wire holder only to plop them with great care into the pools of color. Each boy is allocated one dozen eggs. My husband and I share a dozen. Often this process yields a cracked egg or two.

What a sight to behold: the five of us huddled around the kitchen table without a pepperoni pizza in the middle. This doesn't happen often. Nowadays, for this group to sit in the same place at the same time, the enticement has to be huge. Normally my team of three sons/one husband is off doing their own thing: soccer practice, mowing the lawn, playing video games, maybe some homework. But for these few minutes in April, we gathered as a family with a common goal—to create the best, most bizarre-colored Easter egg.

At my house, best isn't defined like it might be by the judges who award Nobel Prizes or Oscars. You won't find my guys trying to produce a Fabergé egg lookalike. Best usually ends up being the funniest, stupidest, or oddest egg. I suspect that if I had daughters instead of sons, the winning egg might have a more artistic tilt. Alas, as a boys-only mother, I've learned to look at things from a different viewpoint. I stay competitive by marking my eggs with corny sayings or kooky nicknames, but I know I won't win. This contest is fixed. The brothers will vote for each other's entries and I'll end up looking for a recipe that calls for forty-eight hardboiled eggs, give or take a cracked few.

Teasing, pestering, and bestowing nicknames on their loved ones is one way the male species shows they care about each other. Nick was renamed Scoop, after the boys found out he worked scooping ice cream as a teenager. I've been pegged Pebbles, a la the Flintstones' daughter, because of the ponytail I pull to the top of my head when I do my morning workout. During the two years he wore braces, Seth was called Sid (after the mean brace-faced kid in *Toy Story*). All these names and more float to the top during this creative free-for-all, only to find themselves written on eggshell surfaces with a wax pencil the size of a golf tee.

I don't ponder the absurdity of it all, because if I did, I'd be tempted to trade the bags of jellybeans in for green bean seeds and spend the time planting in my garden. Why dye dozens of eggs, put cellophane grass in the bottom of a long-handled basket or buy yellow marshmallow-shaped peeps? Because those things, along with a new dress to wear to church, singing "Here Comes Peter Cottontail," and tulips decorating the center of my dinner table make my Easter.

After inventorying the selection of colored eggs nestled in our refrigerator, the Bunny will place one in each basket to be hidden. On Easter Sunday morning, it will be easy for me to find mine. I'll look for an egg that says "Pebbles Rocks" scrawled unevenly across a purplish tint. That's when I know, ridiculous or not, these are the moments that mean the most. Maybe not to my kids, but definitely to a bonnet-wearing little girl who years later became a mother.

A Pillowcase of Costumes

"What are you going to be for Halloween?"

It's the most asked question during October. At recess, in between soccer drills, or on the drive to piano lessons, you hear preschoolers and preteens alike eagerly pondering the possibilities.

At my house, there was always a lot of discussion before the Halloween dress-up decision was made. Like every other three- to thirteen-year-old, my sons took their time making this important selection. Woe to the kid who chose too quickly and settled for something simple like a pirate, a cowboy, or a vampire.

The chatter started weeks before October 31. Numerous ideas would be kicked around, debated and considered. Like most busy mothers, I did my best to sway the conversation in the direction of accessories we had on hand (cowboy hat, black cape, baseball mitt). I cheered when one of the younger siblings wanted to be what their big brother was last Halloween.

This particular mid-October, my family was busy unpacking the Halloween gear; boxes filled with decorations as well as leftover bits and pieces from Halloweens past. Shawn (11) and Jake (7) were carefully inventorying what items might work for this year's costumes. Mingled in among the seasonal supplies—a glow-in-the-dark skeleton, pumpkin carving knives and fake fangs—were three hollow plastic pumpkins the boys used the previous year for trick-or-treating.

"These are way too small," Jake complained as he pulled them out of the box. "All my candy falls out."

I had to agree. The previous year he and big brother Shawn walked every street and cul-de-sac within a mile of our home; their dad and I, pushing two-year-old Seth in the stroller trailing behind. By the time we turned for that final stretch home, Jake's hand was spread across the top of his trick-or-treat bucket, making sure none of his treasure spilled out.

"Can we get bigger bags this year?" he asked.

Nick, remembering his own candy-collecting pursuits, said his mom let his brothers and sisters use pillowcases. With some reluctance I went to my linen closet and fished out three of my sturdiest white pillowcases to donate to the cause.

"They're so plain," grumbled Jake when I handed them over. "Can we paint them?"

Before I knew it, brushes, poster paint and markers had been dragged out from the craft box. The Halloween décor was pushed aside while energetic artists set to work. Ghosts, pumpkins and goblins took shape on the canvases. Not sure what all the excitement was about, Seth did his best to join in the fun. As the painters worked, the conversation returned to the original question: What can I be for Halloween?

When my sons were little (under 4), the dialogue was brief. At my direction, they each took a turn being a cheetah, Robin (of Batman and Robin fame) and Davy Crockett (costumes inherited from older cousins). But now I had to run down the list of available options (available meaning that I had all the parts) for Jake. The list was varied but not remarkable; firefighter, baseball player, zookeeper. It amounted to an inventory of the costumes Shawn had worn.

Listening as I recited his Halloween history, Shawn grabbed a marker and started writing the names on the back of his newly acquired candy bag/pillowcase. His nine entries included masquerading as a traffic light in first grade and as a killer tomato in third grade (although, to his great disappointment, most treat-givers mistook him for a giant pumpkin).

Jake joined in and printed his shorter list of names. A few minutes later, after much deliberation, Shawn added the words Incredible Hulk to his list, Jake wrote ninja turtle and I penned zookeeper on Seth's sack. From then on, the guys recorded each year's costume name on their pillowcases before setting out for trick-or-treating. They'd return home with pillowcases bulging from their caches of candy bars, lollipops, gum, coins, and the toothbrushes given out by Frances, our neighborhood dental hygienist.

That year, I abandoned my quest for recycling costumes, and the boys' imaginations blossomed. In the Halloweens that followed, a new stream of characters came to life. Visits to costumes shops, thrift stores and bargain bins yielded disco-era bell-bottoms, light sabers and tie-dyed shirts. And character names like Indiana Jones, Harry Potter, "Disco Dude" and "Hippie Guy" were carefully inscribed on what would become three family heirlooms.

These linens, still part of our Halloween décor, are unpacked every October and displayed near a table that holds a treat-filled black cauldron, a jack-o-lantern and a ceramic ghost. Three somewhat shopworn pillowcases that chronicle a time when at least one six-year-old boy thought being Buzz Lightyear was cool and that a handful of Tootsie Pops was a prize to behold.

Thinking Thankful

About six years ago, I began keeping a gratitude journal. My notebook is nothing fancy. It's a simple black-and-white speckled composition book. I buy one for less than $2 every year at the back-to-school sales. On those lines, I jot down at least three things each morning that delighted me the day before. It's a great way to begin each day, spending a few minutes thinking about what I'm grateful for.

The daily demands of being a wife, mother, friend, and consumer (just to name a few) offer us lots of opportunities for disappointment, challenge, and frustration. By taking a moment to reflect on what's gone right the day before, you can give yourself another opportunity—one that adjusts your view to see the glass as half-full instead of half-empty.

Through sleep-rimmed eyes, before my feet hit the floor, I reach for my journal, stationed on my nightstand, and start writing. Some entries are simple one-word notes like "sunshine," "reading," or "bargains." Others are short prayers of thanks for my family's good health, the addition of a new niece or nephew or making it through a tough time.

Longer passages are a bit more reflective. They may boast the success of one of my sons, record my feelings about a recently published article or pat myself on the back for achieving a small goal—cleaning out a closet. I'm reluctant to admit that there seems to be a disproportionate number of entries involving food—lunches with friends, family dinners, new recipes that worked, a surprise dessert.

These pages are my paper sanctuary; a place to preserve the positive. They are a way to slow down my mind and reflect on the good news in my life. It's what I call Thinking Thankful. Focusing on the good stuff that happened the day before lessens my usual spinning about things that normally make headlines in my mind—the computer crashing, the mess in the family room, a window screen chewed by our dog Max, or a rejection slip from an ill-informed editor.

A wide variety of subjects can find their way into my gratitude journal, many more than just the three entries I typically cover. Some days I take the time to write more, but knowing that I only have to come up with three makes it easy to fit this appreciation review into my morning routine.

Some items that show up with regularity are ways to simplify life. Great ideas from friends—like the ideal construction of a peanut butter and jelly sandwich. My recipe was two slices of bread, one slice slathered in peanut butter, the other in jelly. It wasn't until lunching with my friend Rik that I learned the faultiness of my formula. As he ate his lunch, I noticed that his sandwich didn't have that "grape-jelly seepage" mine were famous for. Rik covers both slices of bread with a thin layer of peanut butter and then jellies in between. Perfect PB and J every time.

It's also important to me to read what I've written weeks or months before. A year ago I was happy about yoga stretches, helping my son Jake fill out college applications and a Sunday morning visit with my mom. Today I'm still doing my morning yoga, Jake's a freshman in college but the chances to see my mom's angelic smile ended last September. My journal lets me note what I might take for granted and is a record for how quickly life changes.

Because of my early morning writing practice, I'm actively paying attention to the good stuff that life sneaks in when I'm not looking. I stop to think about what went right during the last twenty-four hours. Little things like my husband starting a load of laundry; my sisters, Sadye and Sue, tracking down hard-to-find books for me at their neighborhood used book stores; a friend dotting my desk with ladybug stones the size of dimes, just because she knows I like ladybugs.

None of these things are life-changing. They're not life-altering events like winning the lotto, paying off your mortgage, or finding the perfect job. Fortunately, though, they are life-enhancing. Taken together, they comprise the best parts of living. These are moments I might miss. I might take them for granted if I wasn't writing them down.

Today's technology lets us accomplish more in less time. That should be a good thing, but instead, we're moving at the speed of life, going faster and doing more. Sandwiched between laundry, homework, and grocery shopping, there's little space left to ponder and contemplate.

There's lots of good stuff sprinkled throughout the day. Jot some of it down. Remembering what you're thankful for savors today's journey, regardless of tomorrow's destination.

Sitting at the Big Table

As November 27th gets closer, lots of us are spending time in preparation and anticipation. We're busy comparing prices for frozen turkeys, finding grandma's recipe for cranberry sauce and ordering chiffon pumpkin pies. We've assigned a favorite aunt the task of bringing the green bean casserole and asked our neighbor if he has folding chairs we can borrow. All of this organization is necessary to carry out our vision of the perfect holiday dinner; one that merits a symphony of satisfied after-dinner sighs that continue long after the wishbone has been pulled. But to me, these details are secondary. While many of you are dusting off your crystal and sharpening the carving knife, my energies are spent on how to fit nineteen seats and a highchair at a table that comfortably accommodates ten.

Everyone who's coming to Thanksgiving dinner at my house sits at one table, no matter how long, awkward, and cumbersome that table turns out to be. Some therapists might consider this fixation of mine a character flaw, one that traces its beginnings back to my childhood. An unnecessary expenditure of energy that I should have resolved over the years. "Just set up an extra table for the kids," they would advise, "and don't worry about it." But I do worry and I worry a lot.

I'm the youngest of four children. The baby of the family. Over the years, I've been placed at the children's table a time or two, or twenty. And to this day, I'm still a bit sensitive about where I sit during holiday meals. So much so, that when Thanksgiving or Christmas dinner is held at my house, I make every effort to link as many tables as it takes for everyone to sit together. The banquet often spans the length of my dining room and encroaches well into our kitchen/TV room.

Why such a campaign against a kids' table? It has a lot to do with the age span between my older siblings and me. Some say I was a surprise addition, born about a dozen years after the then-youngest, Paul. My brothers and sister are more than a decade older than I am. It's no wonder that they've treated me like a child instead of a peer. So, when the seating at the dining room table became snug, it was easy for Mom to demote me to the kids' table to feast with my nieces and nephews.

Sitting at a card table or a coffee table located closer to the garage than the formal dining room magnified the fact that I wasn't on the A (adult) list. The "kids" were out of earshot of the grown-ups. I couldn't hear what they were talking about, but I knew it had to be better than discussing Casper the Friendly Ghost cartoons or Romper Room's magic mirror.

My complaints fell on deaf ears. "You're going to eat the same things we are," came the calming retort. It didn't matter. I was still ticked. This was an unfair division of family. I wasn't one of the kids, even though I was 11 (technically eligible for the child's discount at the movies). I was Aunt Claire. So what if I was barely five years older than my oldest nephew—I was still an aunt, not a child. I demanded the status that was rightfully mine.

I wanted to sit at the table with the stemware, not the Tupperware. To be closer to the turkey platter and gravy boat than the chocolate milk and bibs. I envisioned myself eating off the nice plates and drinking my apple cider out of a goblet instead of a jelly jar. At least that's what I claimed.

Truth be told, mostly, I just wanted to be near my big brothers and sister. They were grown and out of the house. Their lives were busy, raising families of their own. On these special days, they were back home and I wanted their attention. I wanted to fit in with the adults. I was too young to know that time passes quickly and once you've grown up, you're an adult for a long, long time. Sitting at the kids' table might not have been such a bad thing.

Fortunately, the emotional scars I've endured from the years of sitting at the little table were fleeting. At holiday meals, I now focus on happy moments like, "Who ate the marshmallows off the sweet potato casserole?" On occasion, I've even fought back the urge to seat my siblings at a rickety folding table near the refrigerator.

We youngsters previously seated at the kids' table now have children of our own. The dilemma of making room for everyone continues to challenge my creativity. I hold fast to my desire for us all to be at one long, connecting surface, even if that means bringing the redwood picnic table in from outside. But there are no complaints. Any day that finds me surrounded by more family than I have chairs to accommodate is a day that I happily give thanks.

Messing With Tradition

I haven't told my kids yet, but I'm adding a new side dish to our Thanksgiving Day feast. I'm hoping to slip this small change through without any notice. It's risky, I know. "Leave well enough alone," my mom would have advised. "Don't fix something that's not broken. Why mess with tradition?"

Tradition, tradition! The song from *Fiddler on the Roof* rings in my ears. Tradition! Is that just another word for expectation? Because I know that my sons Shawn, Jake, and Seth count on certain things to happen on Thanksgiving Day. For them and their dad, the elements are simple and immutable: watch football, throw the ball around during half time, eat roasted turkey, pat their overfilled tummies and doze on the couch. I'm not crazy enough to change any of that.

My kids like everything the way it is—the way it has always been—the way they remember it when they were little. They don't react well to change when their dinner, especially Thanksgiving dinner, hangs in the balance.

But this November they're in for a surprise. I'm not considering replacing the turkey with moo goo gai pan or swapping the pumpkin pie for tofu tarts. I won't commandeer the remote to watch an all-day *I Love Lucy* telethon.

Even though my planned improvement is minor, I know that I'm tempting fate. Every smart woman realizes that you don't mess with the status quo. That the meal you serve on Thanksgiving Day is sacred.

I get that. Some important things should stay the same. We find perfection in saying the Pledge of Allegiance, passing out cigars (real or bubblegum) to welcome a newborn or watching the New Year's Eve ball drop at Times Square. We are comforted by what we know, what's familiar, what's customary. We thrive on the routine and the expected.

I have no beef with Thanksgiving traditions. I have a few of my own, like sifting through the "day-after" sale ads in preparation for an early-morning shopping spree, or eating apple pie for breakfast the next day. But sometimes you just gotta break the mold. Open the window to let in a fresh breeze. Shake the moths out of your Irish linen. What's wrong with adding something extra to a holiday famous for herb-scented stuffing, wishbones, and counting blessings?

Our once-a-year-on-a-Thursday banquet will basically be the same. I'll still bake Sadye's sweet yeast dinner rolls. Nick's creamed carrots will find a corner of our dining room table. Aunt Sue will bring her to-die-for mashed potatoes. The candied yams (more candy than yams) will be stationed near Seth.

I promise not to take away any of foodstuffs that are ingrained in our family's history. Except maybe the cranberries (no one ever eats them anyway) and replace that slot with Watergate Salad. Okay, I've said it. This is all about me wanting to squeeze into our already bountiful Thanksgiving spread a concoction of whipped cream, pistachio pudding, pineapple, and mini-marshmallows.

Who doesn't love this fluffy confection? I'd forgotten about this delicious dessert until a month ago when I enjoyed some at a friend's house. My mom used to make it on hot summer days, special occasions, or pretty much whenever the mood struck her. Watergate salad wasn't a part of any formal tradition, but it's a comforting edible memory of my childhood. Its flavor reminds me of when she was the one swirling around in the kitchen instead of me. I can still hear her singing "When the Saints Go Marching In" above the whir of the electric mixer as I waited to lick the beaters. Florence Yezbak's favorite salad needed to be chilled, but my memories of her are warm.

So maybe this menu renovation isn't about starting something new. It's more about reviving something old. A recipe that takes me back to when my mom was in charge and the only thing this little girl had to do was find her spot at the table.

I'm not so different from my kids after all. I like things to stay the same. I feel safe when my family is gathered around the way they used to be. And even though life changes, thankfully I have a dinner table that expands to accommodate even those who can no longer be here. There's always room for family and friends, favorite recipes, new traditions. And if a bowl full of fluffy pale green pudding can bring back special memories of yesterday, then all I can say is: move over, green bean casserole!

Tilting the Tree
(and other slanted celebrations)

Christmas season starts at my house when the tip of a just-cut pine tree points to the corner of our living room ceiling. Each year, my three sons and I stand in amazement as their father once again puts up our Christmas tree at an angle. We're not sure how Nick manages this feat, because the tree always stands perfectly straight when they drill it at the Christmas tree lot. Somehow, during the ten-minute drive from the Bonita Pinery to our house, the tree transforms into a diagonal demon.

We fought this laid-back appearance. None of us went along willingly, wanting to accept a leaning tree. Year after year, we denied reality, until finally Seth stated the obvious: "No matter what tree we picked, it leans a lot like that tower in Italy."

In Decembers past we'd meet the tilted-tree challenge with renewed vigor, each of us committed to making the tree stand straight. We wanted it pointing skyward, gracefully framed by our picture window, reminiscent of that tower in Paris. The five of us circled the tree, each with our own viewpoint. And not until we each declared that the tree was standing erect would Nick give the go-ahead to the tree lot attendant to drill. Each year this collection of pine needles, branches and sap outsmarted us.

Last year we conceded defeat. "So what if the tree is a bit off center," Shawn said. "It's not the tree's fault. Maybe the living room floor is uneven," Jake added,

handing me a pile of holiday books. "Let's just prop it up."
The good news is the tree stands straighter, but bad news is
that we can't read *Polar Express* or *Olive the Other
Reindeer* until after January 1.

Tree-tilting isn't the only Fadden-specific tradition
that manages to amaze, confound, and delight our holidays.
My top five include:

1)   sending Christmas cards to people who don't
send ones to us;

2)   receiving cards from everyone I didn't send a
greeting to;

3)   being one egg short for that last batch of sugar
cookies;

4)   a size 10 shoe stepping on my most treasured
and breakable ornament

5)   and the never-untangling string of lights.

As illustrious as these five are, tree-tilting is still our
most beloved. It's the one I know my sons will someday
tell their children about. In the years to come, they won't
remember the Game Boys, DVD players, and new clothes
that were opened through sleepy eyes. But they will
remember the effort we shared to display our tree
vertically.

I dread the thought that Nick might put the tree up
straight one year. Then I'd be forced to search for a new
family favorite; perhaps burning the sugar cookies or
hanging advent calendars that don't have chocolate in
them.

December days continue to include baking cookies,
hanging stockings, singing carols, spending too much on
presents, and overeating. Every decoration, string of lights,
and Christmas puzzle is still dragged out of the garage and
displayed before Shawn, Jake, and Seth officially declare
Christmas underway.

But it's the traditions my family embraces without
realizing it that mean the most, the ones that burrow their

way in without any masterminding. Tree-tilting is an annual event we hadn't planned on, but now it's as much a part of our holidays as leaving cookies for Santa and carrots for the reindeer.

And for a mom who's always organized, I take joy from these unexpected and random life events. Those vivid memories of sights, sounds, smells, and touches that we warmly recall as adults. My imagination wanders back to my tattered red stocking hanging from the mantel. Each year it cradled an orange, a few walnuts, and a candy cane (Mom's threat of getting a lump of coal never materialized). There's the smell of Sitie's bread coming from the kitchen and albums showcasing photos of smiling (and crying) kids sitting on the laps of varying-shaped Santas.

This holiday season as you gather your family to celebrate your traditions, be on the lookout for those hidden moments; the ones that aren't planned or arranged. Those are the ones supplying the most giggles, hugs, and happiness, the stuff of happy childhoods.

And as you hang mistletoe, pour another cup of eggnog or put the star on the top of your tree, remember that somewhere in California, the annual "tilting of the Christmas tree" is taking place. Maybe this year I'll use a few back issues of *Writer's Digest* to help straighten things out.

From the Kitchen of...

It's not fancy. It uses five ingredients, and you won't find it in *The Joy of Cooking*. Still, "Aunt Sadye's Mac and Cheese" is the #1 most requested meal in my home. I've served it over and over since my sister Sadye first shared it with me years ago. It had been her son Thomas's favorite dinner. I know the recipe by heart, yet I pull out the card—tattered and oil-stained—and read the directions written in her hand.

Eager to help a young bride on the road to becoming a good cook, my sis had tucked a blank recipe card inside each invitation to my bridal shower. Along with dishtowels, waffle irons, and food processors, guests supplied me with their family's treasured recipes. I keep this personalized cookbook-in-a-can on a shelf near my stove in the Favorite Recipe file Sadye also supplied. Some recipes I've mastered: Chocolate Refrigerator Cake (Sara), Meat Loaf (Carole), Hummus (Mom), Stew (Melissa), Refried Beans (Cara), Chinese Chicken Salad (Sue). Some I didn't: Cioppino (Mary), Chicken Kiev (Laura).

During the hustle and bustle of a normal week— when the goal is nutritious, plentiful and fast—I turn to online recipe sites to expand my menu options. Quick dinners like spaghetti chicken, sloppy joes, and taquito casserole satisfy the hunger pangs of my husband Nick, my sons, and any of their friends who may be loitering around the house at dinnertime. Over the years, a few of those meals-in-minutes made it into our family's food hall-of-fame recipe file.

At the start of the holiday season, I comb through this handpicked collection searching for Christmas cookie ideas. Maybe this year I'll try Jane's Chewy Rolo Cookie Bars or Elena's Snickerdoodles. I reacquaint myself with the secret ingredients in Sweet Sue Potatoes. Most hummus dip recipes call for two cloves of crushed garlic, but Mom always added an extra clove or two, so I always double-check my garlic supply. I pull out the Chex Party Mix recipe, complete with hand-written additions, critiques and requests: add flaming hot Cheetos, no peanuts, less wheat Chex, more almonds, and pretzel sticks. Throughout the month of December, disappointed faces would multiply if bowls of the crunchy stuff didn't dot the end tables and countertops of my home.

Right after Halloween, my shopping list fills up with items purchased only once a year (garlic bagel chips, pistachio pudding, red food dye, mini-marshmallows, yams) to prepare the dishes my sons eagerly anticipate and come to expect in November and December. The guys aren't overly attached to noodles, cheddar cheese, or green beans and crunchy onions. It's the scents, the textures, and the flavors of the holidays they're anticipating—the ones that don't feel or mean the same in March or September. Whether we're curled up on the couch watching *Miracle on 34th Street* or gathered around the dining room table giving thanks, our taste buds savor the cuisine, but our hearts crave the memories.

These are the moments when we're cooking more than sustenance. Eating is more than nourishment. Food and how it's prepared is handed down mother to daughter, sister to sister, friend to friend. Complicated meals that we don't find time to prepare on a lazy summer day are the focus of December afternoons. Families gather to assemble tamales using Grandma's traditional recipe. Batches of breakfast strata are whipped up effortlessly.

The womenfolk in my family schedule an annual baklawa-making event at my niece Denise's home. (The Greeks call this decadent dessert baklava.) We spend hours chopping pistachios, tediously hand-brushing paper-thin phyllo dough and gingerly layering the nut, sugar, and cinnamon mixture in between the flaky folds. By the time honey is poured over the diamond-shaped slices and trays of the rich pastry are popped into the oven, generous helpings of laughter, wisdom, and love have been exchanged.

With a little effort, homespun recipes transform into a gourmet diary, a family food history. All the shopping, the measuring, the tasting, and the smells are recorded on 3x5 index cards, that begin *From the Kitchen of...* and end with *...serves 4-6*. They're written by Grandma, a special aunt, a niece, a brother, a godmother, a long-time friend. This tried-and-true formula ultimately combines to satisfy hearts as well as tummies.

Maybe I'll make a memory tonight, starting with Mom's hummus. Hope I have enough garlic.

Piecing Things Together

Forrest Gump compared life to a box of chocolates. I'm a chocolate lover (especially when it's covering nougat), but I disagree. I think life is more like a box of jigsaw puzzle pieces—1,000 lopsided segments, odd-shaped bits, and unfamiliar parts. Some pieces are smooth and easy to recognize; others are downright jagged and unwieldy. You know it's going to take a while to figure out which side is up. Like many moments in life, puzzles start out a jumbled mess, but with consistent effort, piece by piece, it all comes together. Fun, frustration, and unexpected surprises intertwine as the fuzzy picture comes into focus.

I've been a jigsaw puzzle aficionado since I was a teen. You'll find one, in various stages of completion, atop my dining room table. I keep it corralled on a sheet of foam-core board for easy relocation to a coffee table when it's time to eat. Visitors—family and friends—are familiar with my loosely enforced ten-piece minimum. Before kicking up their feet, getting a snack out of the fridge or changing the TV channel, they're invited to make a puzzle contribution. After all, we're in this together.

My three sons grew up with jigsaw puzzles in their midst, but only two share my puzzle passion. The oldest, Shawn, displays remarkable patience as he methodically matches pieces to the correct opening. He likes to work in quadrants. Youngest brother Seth declares his preference to work in silence, not appreciative of the ongoing banter between Shawn and me during the puzzle-resolving process. Middle son Jake doesn't work at all. He's a puzzle-giver, opting to gift them rather than complete them. Thanks to Jake, hours have been spent reconstructing movie posters, scenes from TV sitcoms, carousel horses, and—my favorite—the impossible sea of dice.

All were challenging, but not as dangerous as the puzzle my friend Robin loaned me—a plate of Oreos. Ten days, three empty cookie bags and two pounds later, it was complete. When I returned it, traces of black cookie crumbs that had fallen from the corners of my mouth were mixed in with the pieces.

Our family comes from a strong line of mystery-solvers and puzzle-doers. When my sons were little, their grandfather Tom helped them complete their 100-piece preschool puzzles, insisting they put the frame together first. An engineer by trade, Pop never consulted a dictionary as he solved newspaper crosswords in ink, a feat I've never attempted. We still follow Pop's frame-first jigsaw puzzle tradition. I think he'd forgive us the occasional slip when eager hands finish a section before all the edge pieces have been ferreted out.

Not only are jigsaw puzzles a spontaneous, ongoing way to spend snippets of quality time together, they can aid in untangling some of life's quandaries: Why does the internet disconnect when the house phone rings? How can I camouflage the leftover meatloaf? What's that weird hissing sound in my bathroom?

Often, answers don't come easily. Instead of racking my brain, I work puzzles. In the quiet early morning, under the bright illumination from my skylight, my brain clears while I make sense out of a jumble of pieces. Previously unrelated colors and shapes slowly form a cohesive picture. Remarkably, other life concerns find their solutions as I search for edge pieces or one that resembles a shamrock.

Sprinkled among this season's holiday cookie-baking, present-wrapping, and tree trimmings will be Christmas-themed jigsaw puzzle-solving. I can't wait to open the classics we work each year like the Norman Rockwell holiday montage or Charlie Brown's Christmas tree. With holiday busyness surrounding me, puzzles are a delightful break from the frenzied action. They're my pause in the midst of competing deadlines.

I've learned my lesson, though. This December, when I'm shopping for a new puzzle to add to the collection, I'll bypass the lids picturing gingerbread men, candy canes, and chocolates. I'm sticking with peaceful, joyous, festive images—snowmen, carolers, and angels—whose charms won't compromise my waistline.

Cookies for Conversation

A cozy circle of about twenty friends crowd into my living room, each selecting a small wrapped gift from a nearby pile before finding a seat. We've spent most of the last hour in my kitchen chatting and sampling the potluck offerings. The taste of orange chicken, artichoke-spinach dip and grape leaves, still a recent memory. Cups of sherbet punch and a few glasses of something a bit stronger dot the end tables. The coffee is brewing.

The reason for this gathering is the annual recitation of *How the Grinch Stole Christmas*. This holiday ritual, the highlight of my cookie and ornament exchange, requires each woman to read a page from the Dr. Seuss classic, then pass the book to her left. The rest of us listen attentively, waiting for the word Grinch to be said aloud. That's our signal to send the present balanced on our lap to the gal seated to the right.

Eventually, every voice is heard and not until after "the Grinch himself carves the roast beast" do we open our gift and delight in a new ornament to hang on our tree. In these few moments, the spirit of the season transforms this room full of moms and grandmoms into children of wonder.

My original intention for hosting this shindig wasn't benevolent and pure, though. It was practical and a bit selfish. I wanted to have an abundance of holiday sugar cookies, fudge, and popcorn balls to serve Shawn, Jake, and Seth, as well as any friends and family who happened by. And I didn't want to have to convert my kitchen into a bakery to accomplish the task.

Fifteen years ago, I borrowed this shortcut-to-homemade-cookies-and-candies from my across-the-miles friend Cyndee. I liked her idea so much, I decided to start my own version. It's a pretty good deal, too. In exchange for bringing three dozen homemade cookies, an appetizer to share (and of course, a wrapped Christmas ornament), I provide the locale, some beverages, and an atmosphere conducive to friendship.

My guest list combines football (baseball, soccer, cheerleading) moms, PTA members, and ladies who know where there's a sale on just about everything. It's not beyond any of us to have twisted an arm or two while selling fundraising candy bars. Most of us have stayed up late gluing the final planet on their kid's science project. On this special evening, however, we put our maternal mojo aside, take off that domestic goddess sash and replace it with an imaginary tiara reserved for wide-eyed lasses.

For three glorious hours, no ref whistles interrupt our conversations. There's no ballet practice. No one needs a ride to piano lessons. You won't find snack bar nacho cheese sauce caked under our fingernails. And nobody's asking the whereabouts of his backpack.

Sure, you might overhear the younger mothers exchanging potty-training tips. It's guaranteed that the boomer moms are showing photos of their grandkids. But for the most part, this night is reserved for the girl-inside-the-grown-up. During weeks crammed with doing for others, this is one thing we gals do for ourselves.

After the laughter has died down, and many hugs exchanged, we get down to our official reason for getting together. Outfitted with smiles and empty trays, the ladies line up to begin a slow parade around my dining room table. It's covered with an array of pecan crispies, gingerbread men, slices of cranberry loaf, and lemon squares. Minutes later, cookie crumbs, traces of powdered sugar, and a few wayward nuts are all that's left. The room is abuzz with excited voices of women ready to take this year's bakery loot home to those folks waiting up for a taste.

I admit that by bribing our families with snickerdoodles, baklava, and brownies, we've gotten away with this boondoggle for a decade and a half. But if this culinary venture buys me a girls-night-in, surrounded by long-time and newly-formed friendships, I'll happily stash an extra bag of flour and some chocolate chips in my pantry. In fact, it's probably not too soon to start testing recipes for next year.

Maybe I should mix up a batch of Jane's Chewy Rolo Cookie Bars, just for research purposes, of course. Gosh, I love the holidays…

Believing in Make-Believe

Every December 24, when Shawn, Jake, and Seth were little, they carefully selected the best-decorated sugar cookies from our day spent baking. Before they went to bed, they placed a plateful of these homemade snacks, along with a glass of milk, near the fireplace for the man in the red suit. Nearby, a bowl of water and a pile of carrots awaited Rudolph and his pals.

Why? Because my sons believed in Santa Claus. They knew that once a year, sometime after they were fast asleep, the jolly old elf would squeeze down our chimney with his sack of elf-made toys to place under our decorated tree. Flying direct from the North Pole, via a reindeer-pulled sleigh, St. Nick also filled their stockings with small goodies and an occasional lump of (bubblegum) coal.

Their innocent belief in the unbelievable didn't just occur in December. The boys spread their faith-in-the-unlikely to other months as well. In March, the Lucky Leprechaun would visit and leave behind a pot of golden candy coins. In the spring, the Easter Bunny bestowed baskets of joy, and in the fall, the Great Pumpkin would come. Not to be left out of the fun, the Tooth Fairy made routine appearances as dental needs dictated.

A bit older now, my sons are still in the business of believing in make-believe. But the trust nurtured in their youth has transferred to everyday items; like the Enchanted

Laundry Chute, the Amazing Self-Stocking Refrigerator and the Incredible Never-Ending Roll of Toilet Paper.

My sons live in the upstairs part of our two-story house. Conveniently located in the hall just outside their bedrooms is the enchanted laundry chute. Behind its hinged gateway dwells a force that draws laundry directly to the washing machine on the floor below. Soiled jeans, gym shorts, T-shirts, and socks dropped down the shaft are whisked into Laundry Never-Never Land. How quickly the enchanted chute works depends on what other demands are made of its mysterious and illusive operator. Typically, within a couple days, contributions are washed, dried and folded. The next time they see their football jersey or soccer uniform, it's clean, folded, and ready to wear.

Our home also possesses a wondrous self-stocking refrigerator. It's not complicated to operate. Thirsty? Open its doors to find an array of chilled juices, milk, or bottled water to quench your parched mouth. Hungry? All the makings for a BLT, a turkey and cheese club, or a quesadilla are at your fingertips. Hankering for a cool snack? Peek in the chamber below (I call it the automatic-replenishing freezer, a kissing cousin to the self-stocking fridge) to find a selection of frozen treats. If you happen to take the last one, simply yell out into the air: "We're out of ice cream!" The Refrigerator/Freezer Fairy will hear your request, no matter where she is or how busy she seems to be. And the next time you reach for a fudgesicle or an ice cream sandwich...*voilá*, it will appear. Harry Potter and his chums at Hogwarts wish they had it this good.

The incredible never-ending roll of toilet paper is monitored by a Paper Pixie, a charmed phantom my sons haven't seen but still believe in. Guarding against the evils of an empty roll on the holder, she commands toilet tissue to appear, so no one is ever left stranded.

Not surprisingly, as they've gotten older, Shawn, Jake and Seth have encountered more bewitched items, enchanted possessions, and unexplained happenings. They've witnessed the Non-Depleting Gas Tank, Mom's (or Dad's) Bottomless Wallet, and the Pantry of Plenty. Max, Baylor, and Bandit, our dogs, are make-believers, too. Daily, they behold the miracle of the Oasis Water Bowl and the Bountiful Doggie Dish. Sons and pets alike don't question where such abundant goodness originates.

I know that my house isn't the only one in the county experiencing these fantasy-like occurrences. That's why, during this season of childhood wonder and surprise, I put my magic wand aside to raise a cup of eggnog in toast to the moms and dads who make these mini-miracles happen. In between sorting the laundry, filling grocery baskets and gas tanks, and kissing boo-boos away, let's take a secret bow for the magic we perform every day.

This Christmas, may your guardian angel keep your teacup full, your sense of humor brimming, and nourish a quiet peace in your heart. And may you and yours always marvel at the make-believe spirit that resides, year-round, in the land of mystery, hope, and love that we call home.

Whose Home for the Holidays?

Ah, love. It starts out innocently enough. You say yes to dinner and a movie. He brings flowers and chocolates. There are romantic walks on the beach. And before you know it, you're married. The days of staring lovingly into each other's eyes are replaced with scanning the food section for bargains, and listening for the sound of the shower turning off so you can take your turn.

You're occupied with many challenges as the two of you begin a life together. So many decisions to make: Cable or satellite? Pepperoni or sausage? Over-easy or scrambled? Foreign or domestic?

Days, weeks, months pass. Miscellaneous facts are gingerly revealed: He likes Brussels sprouts. She thinks birthday cake is a breakfast food. Both of you have trouble staying awake for the eleven o'clock news. Deals are reluctantly made: He agrees to read the sports section until she's finished with the front page. She'll watch *Entourage* if he'll sit through reruns of *The Office*. Then, your newly formed family of two becomes three, four, and maybe even five.

In my case, over eight quick years, the duo of Nick + Claire expanded into a quintet that included Shawn, Jake, and Seth. Of course, more questions arise, more choices need to be made. Cloth or disposable diapers? Public or private school? Guitar or piano lessons? As fledgling parents, we made it through these either/ors while learning about raising sons.

But every November the same question arose; one that never seemed to have an easy answer. Where are we spending Thanksgiving and Christmas this year? At your parents' place or mine?

This guilt-inducing query is best avoided when you're dating. Discuss religion, how you'll vote in the next primary, which pro football team you'll cheer for, but tiptoe around this explosive topic.

Like lots of young couples, we tried to appease everyone by attempting to be in two places at one time. We'd go to my mom's house for an early dinner and his folks' place for dessert. Playing beat-the-clock when Thanksgiving Day is limited to twenty-four hours is tough.

The same is true of Christmas Day. There's not enough time to enjoy the holiday if you're spending most of it crisscrossing the county. We'd barely taste a forkful of candied yams and cranberry stuffing at my mom's table before we were loading ourselves back into the car. I can still hear the voice of a four-year-old Shawn yelling from the backseat as we drove to our next stop: "There goes the pumpkin pies."

In our haste to be on time, the desserts had been set down, but not secured. They slid aimlessly across the van floor and slammed into the back of the front passenger seat, making a gooey-looking burnt-sienna splash across the cloth upholstery.

Scurrying from house to house was how we spent the next several Thanksgivings and Christmases. Inwardly I wanted to mount a stay-at-home-for-the-holidays coup. The thought of packing up three kids, two car seats, a green bean casserole, and sundry other items had lost its appeal. Maybe I had spent too many Christmas Eves staying up until two a.m. helping Nick put together a 350-piece something whose box had innocently cautioned: "some assembly required."

Exhausted toward the end of one of these marathon holiday events, I collapsed on the couch where other similarly fatigued parents grouped. My brother-in-law Leo sitting nearby listened as I lamented the craziness of the season. He smiled and nodded knowingly. His family had just spent their day under similar circumstances.

"Next year, why don't we move our get-together to the day after Christmas?" he proposed to no one in particular. A huge sigh swept through the room, followed by cheers of relief. "Why hadn't we thought of this before?" asked a sister-in-law. "Where does it say that we have to scrunch everything into one twenty-four-hour day?"

The meaningful parts of our celebration would be the same; they would just occur a day later. Pop-pop would still be the center of attention as he donned his Santa hat to pass out gifts. The grandkids would wait, wide-eyed, to hear their name called before eagerly opening their presents. The overabundance of sugar cookies, popcorn balls, and fudge would get a second chance to find a welcome palate.

A once stress-filled, jammed-packed ritual was forever transformed into an extended family-fest. Leisurely, all of us kids-at-heart could delight in the blessings that come when you're part of a large family, minus the harried disposition. No one was keeping an eye on the clock, poised to rush out the door for another gathering. As a bonus, we all got an extra day to anticipate the fun.

I'll spend mine looking forward to a soothing cup of Nana's hot apple cider, a rousing game of charades with the cousins, listening as Uncle George tells us the same old stories—and laughing as though I just heard them for the first time

A Boy, A Box, and Packing Peanuts

The brown box arrived on our front stoop a few days before Christmas. It was from our friends Greg and Jane, who live in St. Louis. The cardboard carton was so big that it took two of us to drag it into the living room. The whole family gathered, anticipating what bounty it held inside. Because of its size, it wasn't a present I could slide near the tree and tell my sons to wait for Christmas morning. This first gift of the season was ready to be enjoyed.

Smiling faces circled my husband as he cut the strapping tape. He reached down through the kernels of packaging to pull out a lavishly filled wicker gift basket. As Nick wiped off a few noodle-shaped foam pieces that clung to the cellophane wrapping, we could see that the basket had treats for every member of the Fadden household. Hot cocoa and biscotti. Smokehouse almonds and sausage. Chocolate-covered pretzels and caramel popcorn balls. Toffee and sugar cookies. And a personalized ornament for our tree.

As Nick and I continued to unpack the basket and review its contents, thirteen-year-old Seth found something else far more interesting than the treasures inside. While Shawn and Jake were busily staking claim to their favorite cookies and candies, Seth had slid the box to the far end of the room and climbed inside.

Christmas at our house was pretty much the same over the years. We hung up chocolate-filled advent calendars; baked sugar cookies shaped like stars, trees and candy canes; put out the carrots for Santa's reindeer. I smile when I think about attending Christmas Eve services and going out to dinner afterward. The boys chattering around the table in an effort to guess what would be inside the one present they'd each get to open later that night. On many Christmas eves, I remember watching the clock hit nine p.m. only to see three little faces lose their fight to stay awake. Eyelids too heavy to stay open had prevailed over their desire to see Santa squeeze down our chimney.

But as Shawn, Jake, and Seth grew from toddlers to boys to teens, some of the holiday magic slipped away. I no longer heard the sounds of their sweet excited voices waking Nick and I up at the crack of dawn on Christmas morning. Now it's more likely to be my voice cutting through the silent house, calling everyone to come and see what the jolly old elf had left the night before.

The morning the box arrived, Nick had commented about how Seth's voice had changed. The high-pitched chiming sound of our youngest son had shifted to the deeper tone of a man-in-the-making. Whiskers had begun to pop out. His once-chubby face was gradually losing its roundness—slimming to give us a preview of what he will look like as an adult. He was already vying for the position of tallest of the three. It wouldn't be long before the phrase "little brother" would shift to "younger brother."

That afternoon, I looked over at Seth-in-the-Box and realized that in spite of all the outward evidence to the contrary, there was still a little boy's heart beating strong inside that big-boy body and it wanted to come out and play.

Before I knew it, the carton, still filled with thousands of white-foam rigatoni-like shapes had spilled (or was spilled) across my living room carpet. Much like a snow flurry, the space between my couch and love seat was turned into a winter wonderland and lying in the middle was Seth. His smile, grinning from the face of a child who hasn't had braces yet, beamed as bright as the North Star. Shawn and Jake, not wanting to miss out on the fun, set aside the gingerbread cookies they were munching and started squishing the foam into makeshift snowballs and pelting each other.

Sure, after the holiday break, everything went back to normal. I suspect that Seth's thoughts returned to studying for his algebra final, wondering what high school would be like and which girls think he's cute. I knew that the run-of-the-mill concerns of teen life would take over for all three sons.

But for a few minutes, on a random December afternoon, the little boy got the better of Seth. Nick and I continued to watch in quiet amazement as he spread a layer of packing peanuts on the floor and lay on his back on top of them. And making the foam popcorn serve as snowflakes, Seth stretched out his arms and legs and flapped them to form a snow angel.

Just like that, with the flutter of a bristly-chinned angel's wings, the magic of Christmas soared back into our home.

A Simpler, Kinder Christmas

No one confuses me with Martha Stewart. I don't get phone calls when a friend wants to create centerpieces using bark, berries, and spray-painted six-pack soda can holders. I wish I were. I know some of those people. They turn a sprig of rosemary, three candles, and a leftover Cool Whip bowl into a sight to behold. I admire them. Everyone looks good in the family photo on their handmade holiday card, even the dog.

I don't know where I was when elegance, artistry, and style were being handed out. I must have been standing in the make-magic-out-of-mushroom-soup line. It's not that I don't admire creativity in others. Just the opposite. I'm the first one to offer a flattering comment. I'll ask the neighborhood artisan what inspired her to place fifty floating candles in the backyard birdbath at the Fourth of July barbecue. I'm not the least bit jealous. I'm realistic. I know that if I re-created the same thing, I'd end up with forty-nine wet candles and a bird on fire.

Still, I try. I want my family to have cozy, pleasant memories of their childhood Christmases. I envision my three sons contently huddled around our hearth, stringing popcorn, and hanging ornaments. Our joyful voices would be singing all the verses to the "12 Days of Christmas" or taking turns reading *How the Grinch Stole Christmas*.

Of course, this will never happen. A more likely scenario is that they are in the driveway, playing basketball and discussing football playoff possibilities while I'm hanging stockings over the fireplace.

Nevertheless, I'm always on the lookout for crafty, memory-making activities that bring a loving family together. That's why an ever-growing pile of easy-to-make holiday craft instructions inhabits a corner of my TV room. There are piles of pages I've collected from numerous issues of *Family Circle, Better Homes & Gardens* and *Good Housekeeping*. The only thing larger than this stack is my intention to actually make one of these projects, one of these years.

It doesn't get much better in the cooking and baking department. Whenever I'm in charge of roasting the big bird, I call my sister, Sadye (the former home ec teacher), for a quick lesson in stuffing preparation and a refresher on how to truss a turkey. My gingerbread house, complete with gumdrops and licorice, is from a kit. I'm a big fan of slice-and-bake cookies. I love the way Santa looks up at you from the center of a sugar cookie.

The fact that I'm artistically impaired hasn't diminished my passion for the holidays. My well-worn DVDs of *It's a Wonderful Life* and *Miracle on 34th Street* are cued up and ready to go on December 1. The cartoon *Frosty the Snowman* is saved until later in the month, along with a fresh box of tissues, because I always cry when Frosty melts.

Luckily, Christmas is not a season reserved exclusively for the creative. It's also for the spiritual, the trusting, and the sensitive. It's for the tranquil, the disorganized, and the easy-going. So, I've made peace with the fact that my home, complete with the artificial scents of pine and peppermint wafting through my kitchen, will never be a model for a Norman Rockwell-esque illustration. My somewhat tilted tree, decorated mostly with kindergarten art projects, won't be featured in the Christmas issue of *House Beautiful*. And it's okay.

This year, I've committed myself to a simpler, kinder Christmas. I've changed my attitude to embrace a gentler spirit of the season. One that doesn't have me tracking super sales that start before the sun comes up. I won't beat myself up if the cranberries are from a can instead of from the farmers' market. I will not panic if it's December 17 and I haven't mailed all my packages. I will smile as I search for a parking spot at the mall.

Most importantly, I will pay attention to why we're celebrating. I will enjoy the moment, whether it's with linen napkins and fine china or paper towels and foam plates. The holidays are for being with family and friends. A time to honor your faith and reaffirm your beliefs. Thank goodness for this pause in the hustle and bustle of life, so that we can recall past Christmases, savor the present moment, and ponder what the future might bring.

As mothers, we hope that our children will reminisce about what Christmas was like at home. That their holiday memories are filled with a magic and a joy that brings satisfied smiles to their faces. Before I know it, my three sons will have their own families and begin their own traditions. It will soon be their turn to share stories about what the holidays were like when they were kids.

Maybe they'll blend into their new life a bit of what they learned from their dad and me. It's guaranteed they won't be passing along my recipe for candied yams.

What A Bargain

It's January 2. My husband, Nick, is standing in our driveway, taking down the last string of lights woven through our bushes. He's carefully wrapping them around a cardboard holder, one strand at a time. His goal is to prevent the lights from being tangled when he gets them out next winter. Fat chance.

Me, I'm inside the garage, packing up the last of the stockings, ornaments, and candles, and squeezing them into one of the eight boxes of Christmas decorations we've accumulated over the years. Our sons are nowhere to be found. Nick's secretly hoping that I haven't added any boxes to the tally this year. Of course I have and I'm hoping he won't notice.

I'm also hoping that come December, I will remember where I put the Christmas cards I just bought. My bargain cards, purchased at a 75-percent discount, will save me a ton—if only I remember that they're in box six of eight. I make a mental note to write that down somewhere. I never do.

That's part of my problem with saving money. I need to be more organized.

I fare about as well as most in keeping track of things. I make lists, buy in bulk, read the sale ads. Since I come from a long line of savers, I'm used to counting pennies. My mother instilled her thrift gene in me, along with her favorite mantra: Save, save, save. So I recycle bubble wrap, wash out plastic zipper bags and I buy next year's cards at Target's after-the-holiday sale. It's a good thing, as long as I remember where I put them when Christmas season rolls around. With three sons to raise, college looming and a gallon of gas topping what I made per hour as a 17-year-old part-time shoe clerk, I have to shop smart just to break even.

That's why I relish the start of a new year. January gives me a clean slate, a fresh beginning, a chance to improve on a few things like spending more time with my family, losing weight, reading more, praying more, and saving money.

Over the years, I've had mixed results with two of the five: losing weight and increasing quality family time. I've done better with deepening my faith and reading more. But it's that being thrifty resolution that eludes my efforts every year. I think that's because it's hard to tell whether I'm really saving money or not.

For example, I had to bring a goodie to a potluck brunch with three of my girlfriends. I bought a 12-pack of giant muffins at a warehouse store. At less than 50 cents each, I thought I'd found a deal. But did I? After the brunch, there were eight muffins left over. None of my friends (also struggling with that lose-weight resolution) wanted to take them home. My sons—more the donut-eating type—weren't interested, either, so my bargain muffins sat untouched in the refrigerator, until I finally tossed them out.

Shopping at the local 99-cent store is another one of my great ways to save a couple bucks. There are deals galore, but when I've spent $47 on 47 knickknacks, novelties, and party supplies, I'm hard pressed to explain to Nick exactly what I've saved. "The price is great, but are you buying stuff we really need?" he says, shaking his head while flipping through the channels in search of a John

Wayne movie. "I don't think we can afford for you to save that much."

Still I soldier on, proudly toting my coupon caddy along with my grocery list to Vons, seeking low prices, bargains, and discounts. As the family budget-balancer, I can't give up on trying to save money. Clipping coupons, mailing rebates, and pursuing two-for-one sales are just part of my strategy to be frugal. That's how I can keep potato chips in the pantry, ice cream in the freezer, and toothpaste in the medicine cabinet. Saving money is more than just dollars and cents written in my checkbook. To me it's a quest, a challenge, a mission to complete. Organized or not, I can't concede defeat.

Because I know that in just eleven months' time, Nick and I will once again be preparing our home and hearth for the holidays. He'll be standing in the driveway, strings of red, green, blue and yellow lights forming a spaghetti-like pile at his feet. As he works to free the bulbs loose from each other, he'll be muttering about the flaws in his new tangle-free storage method

Me, I'll be back inside the garage surrounded by eight or ten brown cartons, having a conversation with myself. Now what box did I put those cards in? Didn't I write that down somewhere? Did I even buy Christmas cards last year?

Maybe there should be an addition to my next New Year's resolutions: improve memory. Hope I remember to write that down somewhere.

Acknowledgements

A huge thank you to my husband Nick and my children Shawn, Jake, and Seth, who never complained about having their lives used as fodder for my essays.

To my sister Sadye Yezbak, who saved every column and promoted my work to anyone within earshot.

To Sue Diaz, who believed in me and spent countless hours, bird-by-bird, to move me from a wannabe-essayist to an award-winning columnist.

To Sharon Bay, publisher of *San Diego Family Magazine*, who gave me the opportunity to be read by thousands.

To my diligent and encouraging readers Yolanda Barber, Sharon C. Cooper, and Kim Yezbak. If you only knew how irreplaceable you are to me.

About the Author

A retired team mom and room mother, Claire Yezbak Fadden is an award-winning columnist, freelance writer, and novelist.

She lives in California with her husband Nick, and three dogs, Bandit, Jersey Girl and Bowie. Claire is the mother of three sons and Sitie to Windley, Grace, and Maxwell.

Contact her at claire@clairefadden.com, www.clairefadden.com or follow her on Twitter @claireflaire.

Other Books by Claire Yezbak Fadden

A Corner of Her Heart
Promises to Keep
Ribbon of Light
Maybe This Time

www.ingramcontent.com/pod-product-compliance
Lightning Source LLC
Chambersburg PA
CBHW021924040426
42448CB00008B/899